A Pair of
Bowls

God (Through Michael James)

TABLE OF CONTENTS

DEDICATION

First and foremost I dedicate this book to God. May this book bring glory to Your name in the highest magnitude. Without You I am nothing and without You I am no one. I thank You, Heavenly Father for sending Your only begotten son to die on the cross for my sins. Through that sacrifice I can live for eternity. I could never repay You for all that You have given me, but I promise I will try my best.

I dedicate this book to my Lord and Savior, Jesus Christ. You gave Your life, so that I may live. Thank You for enduring the punishment that I so much deserve. I promise that Your sacrifice will not be in vain.

I dedicate this book to the Holy Spirit. Without You this book wouldn't be possible. You fed me the words that were written on each page of this book. I cannot take any credit for it. Personally, I am not wise nor qualified enough in any way to write this book. I honestly utilized the words provided by the Holy Spirit. Thank You for Your love, forgiveness, patience, and guidance. May God be the glory.

Next I dedicate this book to my lovely mother, Pamela Daniels-James and my sister, Shlon James. You guys are definitely my backbone and motivation for completing this book. I want to thank you both for being my strongest supporting cast with respect to this book. After completing each chapter I sent it to both of you for review. Thank you both for your amazing feedback and helpful criticism. You both definitely pushed me to my full potential while creating this book. Thank you, Mom for bringing The Lord into my life at such a young age. Thank you for being the first one to teach me His principles about anger, patience, forgiveness and love. Thank you, Shlon for being the one to help me practice those principles about anger, patience, forgiveness, and love. Thank you for always being there for me. I love you both.

I also want to thank the rest of my extended family. A special thanks goes out to my grandmother, Pauline Pettway; Nanny, Gene; my Godmother, Renee Daniels; my Godfather, Aaron Daniels; my father, Michael James Sr; my aunts, uncles, and cousins who have been an amazing support system. Thank you also to the Daniels, Walkers, Scotts, Browns, Lucas' and James'.

And I want to thank my teams SITOO Dreams Corporation, Virtual Bay Films and New Kingz Entertainment. Thank you Qawan, Darrell, Chaz, Rashad, Dom, John, Bryan and Dekedrian. I want to thank you all for backing me and for taking various leaps of faith with me. All of you starved with me! It's now our time to eat!

I want to personally thank the great Joyce Meyer and Bishop TD Jakes. During some of my darkest moments, your words brought light into my life. I have learned so much about The Lord from you two. I also want to acknowledge that after attending one of Joyce's conferences I was motivated to write this book. Any honor or glory that I may receive from this book I definitely share with you both. Thank you very much.

Finally, I dedicate this book to anyone who is in an undesirable place in life and is seeking greater. I want to encourage you to trust in God's timing and to remain faithful. The Lord has a great plan for your life. Just trust in it and be patient. I promise that it will be well worth the wait. I want to encourage you to keep fighting and to keep seeking The Lord.

1

HAVE YOU SEEN MY FATHER?

I was walking the streets of my hometown, panicky, searching everywhere. There was a slight breeze maneuvering through the air, brushing against my face with every footstep. As I roamed the streets I saw people of various walks of life. They all came from different ethnicities and upbringings. They all lived different lives, with different motives and goals. One of them has to know, I thought.

The first person I approached was an older man and he turned out to be racist.

"Excuse me, sir, have you seen my Father?"

"No," he said, "and I don't wish to ever see Him or you. I don't like your people, so get away from here."

I said, "You're not making any sense. How can you not like my people? How can you not like my people, when you *are* my people? My Father sent me to find you. He told me that you would be here."

The gentleman replied, "Who is your Father? Does He even know me? How did He know that I would be here? And by the way, I am definitely not one of your disgusting people."

I said, "But sir, we actually have the same Father and our Father is not of this World (Acts17:24). So you better believe that He knows you. He knows you better than you know yourself. He knew you before you were born and He knew that we would meet at this exact moment. He sent me here to speak to you and encourage you to change your racist ways. We are from the same family. Our Father doesn't see a difference in our race, He sees only His beautiful children, His beautiful children whom He created in His own image (Genesis 1:27). So who are we to judge someone by the pigment of their skin? Rejecting someone because of their physical appearance is the same as rejecting our Father himself. By doing this, you are saying that He didn't do His job correctly. So, sir, I ask you again. Have you seen my Father?"

The older man replied, "Look, I love our Heavenly Father just like everyone else and would never question His work. But how can I associate with a group of people who have brought so much pain to the people of my race?"

I said, "If you truly love our Heavenly Father then you will obey His instruction. Our Heavenly Father wants us to follow His lead, and His Word. Our Father says that we should forgive, just as He forgives us

(Matthew 6:14-15). Yes, things have happened in the past between our two races, but if we truly love God, we will obey Him. Forgive the people who were once your enemies, forgive your oppressors, forgive anyone who has mistreated you. I know that you are an elder, so therefore I give you the respect that is due (Leviticus 19:32). But my Father has sent me to correct you. So when I ask you, 'Have you seen my Father?' I am not asking have you seen Him physically. I'm really asking whether you have seen the way He forgives? Every time that we sin, our punishment is supposed to be death. If you had seen my Father, then you would know that He is very forgiving. Every time we sin, He gives us an opportunity to repent. Then He forgives us and never mentions that sin again. And furthermore, if you had seen my Father, you would have seen that my Father is LOVE. Earlier you said that you love our Father like everyone else. If this were true, then you would inherit His love. Through His Love we are able to forgive. Our Father loved us so much that He sent His only begotten son to die on the cross for our sins (John 3:16). Our Father is LOVE and wants us to love everyone. Racism is an issue of the world. Since it is a worldly issue, it means it's not for us to deal with. We are not of this world. Let's our Heavenly Father dismantle the worldly issues that have risen. Our Father is love so let's stop worrying about race-related issues and just love one another. Why does it matter to you if your neighbor is married to a person of another race? Our Father may have intended for these people to be together. Are you wise enough to say that God was wrong for placing these people together? Why does Jesus' race matter to you? Jesus is also LOVE and demonstrated His love every day of His life. Does it really matter if the picture in the church is accurate? What's more important is what the picture symbolizes, which is our Savior. Do you think that if Jesus were a different race than you, that God would no longer hear your prayers? No! It doesn't work like that. God is still there for us and has great plans intended for people of all races. Some of us are so wrapped up in what Jesus looked like that we forget about what He truly means to us. So remember, God loves us and God is Love. Also know that God lives in us so we automatically inherit His love. When we learn about this love, we get to know who He is. If we don't know who He is, then we don't know who *we* are. So one last time I ask you, have you seen my Father!?"

I walked the older man to the center of the street and asked him to wait there.

God, who made the world and everything in it, since He is Lord of Heaven and Earth, does not dwell in temples made with hands. -Acts 17:24

So God created man in His own image; in the image of God He created him -Genesis 1:27

For if you forgive men their trespasses, your Heavenly Father will also forgive you. But if you do not forgive men their trespasses, neither will your Father forgive your trespasses.
-Matthew 6:14-15

You shall rise before the gray headed and honor the presence of an old man, and fear your God: I am Lord -Leviticus 19:32

I continued up the street and saw a homeless man sitting on the curb. His clothes were torn, his body was filthy, and he wore a cologne called stench that made my stomach do back flips. I approached him and asked, "Excuse me, have you seen my Father?"

He replied, "Sorry, kid, I don't know your Father, and probably wouldn't remember him even if you had a picture. Tons of people walk past me all day long and no one ever stops. I have been alone in these streets for over twenty years and no one cares. No one feels my pain or knows what it's like to be me. Do you know what it's like not to be able to hear your own thoughts because your stomach is growling too loud? Do you know what it's like to have a cardboard box as your roof, a raggedy piece of cloth as a front door, and a shopping cart as your closet? Many people walk past me every day and look at me with utter disgust. It's like they take offense at my presence. When they are not disgusted by me, they are either afraid of me or throwing insults in my direction." He paused for a minute and took a breath, then went on. "Sorry to talk your ear off, but I rarely have people actually stop. So I'm taking full advantage of this. Oh yeah, and I'm sorry but I have not seen your Father."

I told the homeless man, "My Father sent me here to speak, provide hope, and encourage you to have faith. I want you to know that contrary to what you've believed, you have not been alone the past twenty years. You are not even alone now. God is always with you, and will never leave you (Isaiah 41:17). I can't relate to what you're going through, but I can relate to your spirit. The same Holy Spirit that I have in me is in you as well. I want you to know that God loves you more than anything. He wants you to seek Him and then believe in the plan He has for you (Lamentations 3:25). He loves you too much not to have a set plan for you during your struggle. But the only way His plan works is if you allow it to. You have to accept God in your life and Allow Him to direct you. Another key thing to know is that we have to be patient like My Father. He is extremely patient and waits for us to accept His plan (Jeremiah 29:11). Let's face it: none of us has ever lived a perfect life. While we make our mistakes, God patiently waits for us to stop being disobedient. The very least we can do is patiently wait for His will to be done and have faith that we will be delivered. Trust that He has something great in store for you. He will bless you in abundance for everything that you once lacked. So, have you seen my Father?"

I then escorted the homeless man to the center of the street and asked him to wait there along with the older man.

The poor and needy seek water, but there is none, Their tongues fail for thirst. I, The Lord will hear them; I, the God of Israel will not forsake them. -Isaiah 41:17

The Lord is good to those who wait for Him, To the soul who seeks Him. -Lamentations 3:25

For I know the thoughts that I think towards you, says The Lord, thoughts of peace and not of evil, to give you a future and a hope. -Jeremiah-29:11

I left the homeless man with the older gentleman and walked across the street toward a teenage girl. She could not have been more than sixteen years old. She wore baggy clothes and her eyes overflowed with tears. I asked her, "Excuse me, have you seen my Father?

She replied, "Sorry, I can't help you, I don't know who your Father is."

I asked why she was crying and she said, "I'm so lost right now, I don't know what to do. I have been pregnant for a month and, truthfully, you're one of the few people that knows. I am petrified of telling my parents; they are going to kill me when they find out. They will probably disown me.

"What about the Father of the baby?" I asked.

Her response was, "What about him? We dated for about eight months, and I thought he was the one. He told me that he loved me! Then when I told him I was pregnant, he broke up with me. He told me that he didn't want anything to do with me or the baby. Do you know what he had the nerve to say next? He told me that the baby wasn't his, and that I probably cheated on him. That hurt the most because he was the only person that I've been with. I saved myself for him and now he is leaving me out for dead with our child. He even ruined my relationship with my parents, kind of. They warned me about him and were adamant about me leaving him. I should have listened. Now I don't have him, and I am going to lose my parents – especially if I tell them about my baby. I literally have no one and I have no clue how to raise a child. How could I be so stupid? I'm just going to fix this myself, walk into this clinic, and get an abortion. That should fix everything."

I said, "You may have not seen my Father, but He has seen you. He knows you very well, and has sent me to you. Look, I know that you're in a scary place in life and there's uncertainty. I would like to inform you my Father is the ultimate comforter. He is always there for us. His love and His will for our lives are second to none. Even though you may feel that you got yourself into this, you don't have to get out of this alone. The way you're going about this situation is all wrong. The pregnancy may have occurred because of a wrong decision that you previously made, but you should know that God knows how to solve our problems, because He is the only answer. God is a deliverer. He will deliver you from what you're going through (Deuteronomy 31:6). You should also note that every life that ever graces this Earth belongs to God. Even the one that's in your stomach (Jeremiah 1:5). He already has a will for that baby's life. So at this moment, if you have that abortion, you'll be besmirching the will of God. Your free will is what got you into this situation, and your actions of premarital sex goes against what God wants. But God is still there for you no matter what, even if your 'parents' disown you. God will never do that. God is our True Parent, so now seek Him and follow His instructions. Have you seen my Father?"

I then took her to the center of the street and asked her to wait there. She stood there alongside the homeless man and the older man.

> *Be strong and of good courage, do not fear nor*
> *be afraid of them; for The Lord your God, He*
> *is the One who goes with you. He will not leave*
> *you nor forsake you. -Deuteronomy 31:6*

Before I formed you in the womb I knew you; Before you were born I sanctified you; I ordained you a prophet to the nations.
-Jeremiah 1:5

I walked farther up the street and ran into this guy who was sauntering and staggering along. His breath smelled of aged whiskey and his words were slurred. I stopped him and asked, "Have you seen my Father?"

He loudly shouted random garbled words that I couldn't make out. From his attire, it appeared that he'd had a good life. I mean he had a business suit on with shiny shoes, and wore diamond-studded cuff links on his shirt sleeves. From this, one would think that he had a well-paying occupation. He also wore a wedding ring, which showed me that he was married. So I asked why he would allow himself to get so drunk. At that moment he seemed to sober slightly, at least enough to give me a coherent answer. "I drink because it makes me feel good. It helps me to deal with my problems, which I have entirely too many of. My wife just left me and took the kids with her. Not to mention that I really hate the career that I'm in. So is that a good enough answer for you as to why I drink?"

I said, "No, it's not a good enough reason. Your drinking to get drunk doesn't benefit you in any way. It only gives you temporary relief or satisfaction. Why would you use a temporary solution to solve an issue that could last your lifetime? This isn't the answer.

Getting drunk isn't going to get you that dream career, and it's definitely not going to bring your family back. My Father sent me to let you know that He is the only way out of this, not alcohol. My Father is the almighty counselor and psychiatrist. Anything that you are going through He can solve, if you allow Him. Sit down on His spiritual couch and vent to Him. From this He will give you the answers and comfort you are looking for. Don't resort to alcohol. It will never end right. Being drunk will make you vulnerable and weak in a moment when you need to be the strongest. When you are drunk you are not in the correct mental state (Proverb 26:9) This mental state allows the enemy to plot against your life. The enemy wants you drunk so he can gradually pull you away from the things that are from God (1 Peter 5:8). It places this doubt, depression, and shame into your life. Instead of turning to alcohol, turn to God. From this I promise that your problems will be solved. God will restore your longing for a family and will land you in a career that gives you that fulfillment. In both situations, He may not give you your family the way you initially want. He may not give you a career that you initially thought you wanted. Whatever His will is, you will soon see that His plan exceeds anything you ever imagined. Now have you seen my Father?"

Then I led him to the center of the street where the homeless man, the older racist man, and the teenager were waiting and asked him to wait there. .

> *Like a thorn that goes into the hand of a drunkard. Is a proverb in the mouth of fools*
> *-Proverbs 26:9*

> *Be sober, be vigilant; because your adversary the devil walks about like a roaring lion, seeking whom he may devour -1 Peter 5:8*

The next person I ran into on the street was a young gang member who had a bandana in his back pocket. "Excuse me, have you seen my Father?"

He told me he hadn't seen my Father. I then told him how my Father sent me to find him. I told him how my Father wanted him to take up a different life. The young gang banger clutched the gun that sat on his waist. He asked which gang my Father was in. I responded to him by saying that my Father wasn't of this world.

I asked him, "Why are you even in a gang? What do you get for this?

He said, "It's more than just a gang to me, this is family. It's the only real family that I have ever had. I mean I have relatives, but I don't have a family. My father was killed during a dice game on the corner of the street. My mother was never home. Growing up, she always worked like three jobs. As I got older she started working less and became strung out on drugs. So I was basically left to fend for myself. I always wanted the whole family thing. I always wanted that unconditional love from someone - anyone – someone who actually cared if I was all right or wanted what was best for me. This is what the gang offers me. It gives me that family and it also gives me protection.

I told him, "Hey I hear you, but you're going about this the wrong way. My Father has sent me to show that you have another family that you don't even know about. This family protects you and is more powerful than any imaginable street gang (2 Thessalonians 3:3). You definitely belong in this family. With this family you are truly valued. You will be pushed to reach your full potential. God does not want you to hang around these thugs, they are a part of a family that want to steal your soul, destroy your life, and kill you (John 10:10). In God's family you see that God is the ultimate protector. Any force that's of this world, He will shield you from. That is if you will allow Him into your life. Have you seen my Father?

I walked with him to the center of the street where the others stood and asked him to wait there.

> *But The Lord is faithful, who will establish you and guard you from the evil one.   -2 Thessalonians 3:3*

> *The thief does not come except to steal, and to kill, and to destroy. I have come that they may have life, and that they may have it more abundantly. -John 10:10*

Across the street I noticed two men having a dispute. One happened to be a preacher and the other was an atheist. I walked over to them and intervened. "Have either of you seen my Father?" Speaking to the preacher I said, "My Father says, that you work for Him," and to the atheist I said, "My Father told me that you don't know Him, but He knows you. He told me to warn you to change that. Mainly because there will come a day where He will no longer know you." They both looked at each other and asked who my Father was.

I addressed the preacher first. I told him that my Father was the greatest teacher ever, and that He was the one responsible for all of our knowledge and wisdom. "My Father is very gracious and appreciative of the work you do," I said. "Every time you share His word and are able to resist the enemy, He is happy. He is also the ultimate giver, He gave you your very gift and anointing to preach (1 John 2:20). Without that, you wouldn't have this job. He wanted me to encourage you to keep listening to Him (James 5:14). Not to mention, let Him lead the way at all times.

Then I reached out to the atheist. Hey I understand that you may not know my Father and you actually don't even believe in Him. I just want to let you know that He is very real and He wants to have a relationship with you. What do you have to lose by believing in Him? Absolutely nothing! Your life can only become greater. He will give you a righteous way of living. A life where you are filled with happiness, comfort, love, joy, wisdom, protection, and the list goes on (Acts 16:31). Please stop me when I mention something bad. You have nothing to lose, only something to gain. Think of it like this: if you die as a believer and God is real then you will go to Heaven. If you die and God isn't who I say He is, then you will still have lived your life as a noble person. Either way it's a win - win. Honestly, with God you never have to worry about *what if*? He is **real** and wants the best for you in life.

The atheist looked at the priest and me and said," I don't know, I still don't believe so I'll take my chances without Him."

I responded by saying, "Because of your free will, you are allowed to make your own decisions. However, I would like to warn you that regardless of your decision you will actually witness God. You will witness His glory, His grace, and His presence. This will happen when the Father sends Jesus back to the earth. Upon His return, every knee will bow and every tongue will confess that Jesus is Lord. I pray that before that time comes, God softens your heart and reveals Himself to you." I then turned to the preacher again and said, "I pray that you stay attached to my Father at all times during your teachings. May the Holy Spirit and the word of God work in your life at a magnificent level. May it provide you with the wisdom and guidance to fulfill your anointing. Always remember to take pride in your job, for you will be judged a little harder by my Father (James 3:1). One last thing that I would like to leave you with is the knowledge that my Father loves both of you." Then I walked them both over to the others in the center of the street and asked them to wait there.

> *Is anyone among you sick? Let him call for the elders of the church, and let them pray over him, anointing him with oils in the name of The Lord -James 5:14*

> *But you have an anointing from the Holy One and you know all things. -1 John 2:20*

> *So they said. "Believe on The Lord Jesus Christ, and you will be saved, you and your household." -Acts 16:31,*

> *Behold, I stand at the door and knock. If any one hears My voice and opens the door, I will come in to him and dine with him, and he with Me. -Revelation 3:20*

> *My brethren, let not many of you become teachers, knowing that we shall receive a stricter judgment. -James 3:1*

I left the group and began walking up the street. Behind me I heard a baby cry. Then the cries were drowned out by the sound of arguing adolescents. In the midst of the arguing adolescents and the crying baby there was a muffled sound struggling to be heard. The muffled sound was a cry for help. It was crying for some assistance, any assistance. I turned and saw a single mother walking with her three children. Under her eyes were bags heavy enough to cause the strongest groceries cart to collapse. Her clothes were dingy and wrinkled. She wore her hair in a pony tail that looked as if it had been tied years before. Loose strands ran away from her scrunchy, as if they had escaped captivity. So I walked up to her and asked her, "Excuse me, miss, have you seen my Father?"

Annoyed, the single mother responded, "What do think? No, I haven't seen your Father. And I haven't seen these kids' father either! I really have my hands full and absolutely no help. There is no one here to help me or provide compassion. Don't get me wrong, I love my babies, but I had a real future ahead of me. I graduated at the top of my class and had a real chance at a future in singing. All of that ended for me when I fell for a guy that I thought was Mr. Right. He abandoned me and the kids. Every day since then I have been stuck raising these kids and struggling financially. By the time these kids are all grown I will be entirely too old to pursue my dreams.

I asked her, "Why do you have to give up on your dreams?"

She said, "I just told you why. These kids require all of my attention. I give them all my attention and I still have a hard time raising them. How am I possibly going to teach my little boys how to be men? That's their father's job! Oh yeah, wait, they don't have a father."

I said, "They *do* have a Father, and their Father is the same as mine."

"What are you talking about?" She said, interrupted me.

I told her, "We have the same Father, and He is the greatest Father any one could ever ask for. He is the one who will help you raise your kids. He is the one who will teach your boys how to become men. This same Father is there for you and your kids at all times. He hears every last one of your cries and wants to help you. The only thing is that He can only help you if you allow Him to. Will you allow Him to? Have you even tried asking Him for help? Growing up He used to tell me that you have not because you ask not. I will also tell you that sometimes asking isn't just enough. Not only should you ask, but you have to actually believe that He will deliver (1 John 5:14). You must have **faith**. With that faith you begin to understand that through this storm, there is sunshine on the other side. With Him you are never alone, He is always with you. Not only is my Father the greatest parent ever, but He is also the greatest navigator. He will be the one who guides you to your promised land. He will never lead you somewhere to be destroyed; there's reasoning behind everything. He also has a solution for your existing problem. I want to tell you not to resent these children because you were unable to pursue a singing career. These kids are a blessing and serve a purpose as well. If God has truly blessed you with a gift in singing, then He will open doors for you to exercise your gift. He gave you this gift because He wants you to use it. Please understand that if He has given you a vision for your singing, then it will come to fruition (Amos 3:7). But it will happen under His timing and when He feels you are prepared. Our Father gives us gifts because they tie into His will for our lives. So when he's ready for us to apply our gifts, we will. This opportunity will exceed any plan that we ever intended for ourselves. So again I ask you, have you seen my Father?"

I walked her over with the others to the center of the street and asked her to wait there.

> *Now this is the confidence that we have in Him, that if we ask anything according to His will, He hears us.* -1 John 5:14

> *Surely The Lord God does nothing, Unless He reveals His secret to His servants the prophets.* -Amos 3:7

Down the street there was a police car parked with its sirens going off. The officer walked a handcuffed man to the car, pushed him inside, and closed the door. I ran up to the squad car and asked the officer to open the door so that I could speak to the arrestee. The officer said that I could talk to him for one minute at most. So I took advantage of that opportunity. I opened the door and asked the handcuffed man, "Have you seen my Father?

He replied, "Who is your Father? I highly doubt that I've seen your Father."

I asked him to tell me about himself and asked why he was being arrested. The man told me that this time he was being arrested for assault. He said he was a repeat offender. He stayed in and out of jail for most of his life, doing everything from assault, robbery, larceny, drug trafficking, etc. After that I asked him what he got out of being arrested so much. He told me that he got nothing from the arrest itself but received a sense of fulfillment from the crimes he committed. He went on to tell me that when he commits crimes, people take notice and he's seen as somebody.

I said, "Look, you are someone without the crimes. You are a child of God, which far outweighs who you are after being arrested. Our Heavenly Father didn't make us to sit in cages like animals. But sometimes it takes just that for Him to reach you. Moments ago you said that you get nothing from being arrested so often. This is a problem in itself. Our Father is a great counselor and communicator. Sometimes our lives are so hectic that we miss out on key moments to communicate with our Father. See? You are in cuffs right now and headed back to jail. At this moment the only one who can bail you out with deliverance from this life is the Heavenly Father. During your various arrests, have you ever thought about using your one spiritual phone call to call God? He answers every time and will proudly assist you. Sometimes, like any other parent, our Father has to discipline us and put us in this time-out. During this timeout, He wants us to learn a lesson from our mistake. In this way our Father will counsel us and help show us how to turn our lives around. It only works if we listen to the advice from our Holy counselor. He wants you to turn your life around.

The handcuffed man said, "That sounds fine and all, but I don't think that our Father will forgive me. I have screwed up too many times. Every time I am arrested I feel as though He doesn't hear me. Can you speak to Him for me because He doesn't listen when I speak? "

I said, "You couldn't be more wrong. First and foremost, our Father is very forgiving. Even when we don't deserve it. He will forgive you for your actions if you sincerely repent. He has never left your presence, so every time you speak to Him, He hears you. Have you ever considered that you might not be listening to Him? That you're too wrapped up living life your way so that you neglect to listen for our Father? So yes, I can speak to Him for you, but for the sake of *your* life, He would rather speak to you Himself. He wants the two of you to build a personal relationship. At the end of the day, when it comes time to be judged I won't be able to alter His decision for you. I won't be able to go to God at the gates and say, 'Hey, God, he's fine; he's with me.' It doesn't work like that. So I want you to truly seek our Father and surrender your life to Him Fully (Romans 12:2). He is waiting by the spiritual phone for you; why don't you give Him a call."

I pulled him out of the car and walked him with the arresting officer to the center of the street and asked them to wait there.

> *We are hard-expressed on every side, yet not crushed; we are perplexed, but not in despair; persecuted, but not forsaken; struck down, but not destroyed. -2 Corinthians 4:8-9*

> *And do not be conformed to this world, but be transformed by the renewing of your mind, that you may prove what is that good and acceptable and perfect will of God. -Romans 12:2*

Then I heard a loud groaning sound from across the street. It was a lady being carried away on a stretcher by paramedics. I approached the lady and asked, "Excuse me, have you seen my Father?"

She faintly said, "Sorry, sir, but I kind of have a bigger problem right now than helping you find your Father. I have a disease that is getting the best of me. The doctors say that there is no cure for my disease and that I will probably die within a matter of weeks. I have so much to worry about. Who's going to be there for my children? Who will pay my left over bills? I'm so scared right now, I don't want to die. It's not my time. Sorry to talk your ear off, but as you can see, I have things to worry about.

I replied "Look, I know you're going through trying times, but I'm here to provide you with hope. I want you to know that my Father has sent me to find you. He knew that you would be here. He wanted me to let you know not to be afraid. My Father is always with you and nothing will ever change that. He is actually the doctor of all doctors (Exodus 23:25, psalm 30:2). Where your personal doctor says that there's no cure for your disease, my Father says He is powerful enough to deliver a cure (Psalm 41:2-3). He has a remedy for you that cannot be found in this world. I also understand that your doctor said that you have a few weeks to live. I know that the idea of dying scares you. My Father wants me to let you know not to be afraid. As long as you have surrendered to Him you shouldn't fear dying. The reason for this is because He sent His only begotten Son to die, so that we all may live for eternity (John 3:16). In addition, I also want you to understand that no matter what, God's Will will be done. So if it's in His will to take us from this earth, we have to accept and embrace it. The death that we may have here will only be temporarily. We will rise again one day in Heaven. In Heaven God has such a better life intended for us. The sickness that you currently have here will not be a factor. In Heaven we will all be healthy, happy, and loved. My Father wants you to just trust Him and to have faith in His Will. He loves you more than you can imagine. It's also possible that His will is for you to live. If that is His will, there is no one or nothing that can change that. My Father is the ultimate healer. By the snap of a finger He can heal anything. I then grabbed the stretcher from the paramedic and walked it over to the group of the people waiting in the middle of the street.

While I was pushing the stretcher to the center of the street, the paramedic grabbed my arm. She asked, "Can your Father really heal anything from anyone?"

"He sure can," I responded.

She removed her sunglasses and rolled up her sleeves, revealing a black eye and bruised skin. She said, "What about a broken heart from an abusive boyfriend? Can He really cure that because that is something that I feel is impossible. I mean the relationship started off great, and he was a true gentleman. Then it's like he turned into a monster. He became possessive, using violence to control and intimidate me. I tried leaving him a couple of times, but it's like he has a spell on me. Every time I try to break away, he comes back asking me to forgive him. He says he didn't mean it and that he can't live without me. After that he promises that it will never happen again, but of course those are just lies. Now tell me how your Father would heal that."

Instantly saddened by her story I told her, "My Father hates to see you going through this. He does not want to see you hurt. My Father would want you to seek Him. He will not only heal your broken heart. He will also shield and protect it (Isaiah 41:10, Psalm121:7). My Father is the ultimate protector. There is absolutely no force that can break past His protection. I want to encourage you to reach out to my Father and listen to His instructions. He will guide you out of your situation. Through His grace you will be granted a better more prosperous life. My Father is also very compassionate. When we are hurting, so is He. He feels our pain, and is more hurt by it than any of us could ever be." I then grabbed her and told her that my Father was there for her. I took her over to the woman on the stretcher and to the crowd of people I had left in the middle of the street.

At this moment I went to a platform and stood on it. I shouted, "Excuse me, I would like everyone's attention for a moment. I bet you're wondering why I gathered you all. Well..."

"He's going to jump!!!" someone in the crowd frantically shouted. Instantly everyone's attention went over to a building where a guy was hanging out of the fourth story window. We all begged and pleaded for the guy not to jump. Our words didn't seem to work, as this man was entirely too irate.

The man in the window shouted some obscenities and said "I'm going to jump! Don't try to act like you care, no one ever cared before. No one cared when I was abused growing up. No one cares that my wife wants to leave me. No one cares that I have five kids and I'm now being laid off from my job! I don't want to live no more! I just want to end this pain! This is the only way!"

I intervened and shouted up at the window, "Sir, from that window can you see my Father? I say this because I assure you that He sees you. Matter of fact, He also hears you and doesn't want you to kill yourself (James 5:4). He loves you. He wants you to know that He cares and has a better plan for your life. The only way for you to receive that better life is by allowing Him to work. You do that by living and accepting His superior plan. He loves you and wants you to put your life in His hands (Proverbs 19:21). From this transition, He will bless your family and your job situation. He will also give you the most prestigious job that you could ever imagine, and that is a position in the Kingdom of God. This job provides you with a 401k plan that you can take advantage of when you retire, right now, and even long after you die (Jeremiah 29:11). Please don't jump! God has a better plan for you and many blessings waiting for you. Just turn your life to Him and you can reap the benefits."

The man began crying hysterically cried and retreated inside. Moments later he walked out the building's front door and joined the crowd in the center of the street.

I stood at the platform again and said, "The reason I've gathered you all is because I want to tell you about my Father. Honestly, He's not only *my* Father, but He is also yours. All day I have placed emphasis on saying "My Father" because I wanted to show the acknowledgement of His presence in my life. Through this acknowledgement I am able to claim Him for who He is. He is truly in my life and I want Him to be in your life also. The next time I speak to you all, I don't want you saying things like, 'I haven't seen *your* Father.' I want you to say, 'I have seen *my* or *our* Father.' I want you to claim our Heavenly Father just as He claims us as His children. I also want to define what I meant by asking, 'Have you seen my Father?' When I proposed this question many of you assumed that my Father was lost. He's not lost at all; He's just misplaced in some of our lives. Through this question I'm not asking whether you've physically seen Him, but if you've spiritually seen Him. Have you seen how He loves us all? Have you seen how much patience He has? Have you seen how He protects and shields all of His children? Have you seen the joy that He exerts? Have you seen how He guides us all? Have you seen how He makes good on all of His promises?

So who is our Father? Some refer to Him flat out as God. He is also referred to as the Heavenly Father, Yahweh, Jehovah. He is the beginning. He is the End. He is the Almighty Creator. He is the King of Kings. He is The Lord of Lords. There is no one higher. He is everything that is great in life. He opposes anything that is negative or evil. He is our Father, Doctor, Teacher, Best Friend, Confidant, Protector, Guide, Deliverer, Shield, Director, Comforter, and I could go on listing things for days. I want you to understand who He is. By knowing who He is, we can then learn who we are. We should know that He is loving, patient, joyful, generous, forgiving, hopeful, and so on. What is amazing about all of these things is that He lives within us. So therefore we inherit a piece of these wonderful traits. These things that reside within us are a gift from God that no one can take away from us. Always remember that because the enemy will try to convince you that you lack something, but this is impossible because through the presence of God in our lives we are fully equipped with everything we need. No one can tell you differently. Through the personality traits that are inside us through God, we are supposed to release those traits and display them to the world. For example, because God is loving, we should exhibit that love everywhere we go. We should try our best to be a walking blessing everywhere we go. Because God is patient, we should exhibit patience everywhere. We should patiently wait for God's Will to be done. We must understand that His timing is superior to ours. He may not work in a time frame that we want, but that's because His timing truly is superior. Since God is joyful, we should be joyful everywhere we go, even when it hurts. The power of our joy is one of our greatest weapons that God provides us with against the enemy. Because God is generous, let's be generous when life calls for it. If we see someone struggling or hurt, let us try to assist him. For instance, when we see someone who is less fortunate, let's try to help that person. Our Father is also forgiving. He will forgive us for our sins and then won't bring them back up. Let's exercise that same forgiveness. Let's forgive the people who may have said something or harmed us, whether it was physically, mentally, or psychologically. Let's forgive them. When we forgive them, it's not only for their benefit, but for ours as well. It takes a lot more energy to hold a grudge than it does to move on with our lives. So let's forgive. When we fail to forgive, our enemy is capable of manipulating us through our minds. And last, our Father is Hopeful. Because He lives in us, we should also be hopeful. Through this hope our Father is able to easily maneuver in our lives and send us blessings. Without hope, we could be blocking our very own blessing. It's imperative that all of you understand that there is no situation that you're going through that God can't deliver you from. It's also imperative that you understand that you don't have to search hard for God. You don't have to search hard because He lives within you. I want you to understand we need Him and cannot do anything without Him. We are nothing without Him. So therefore, in times of trouble, happiness, depression, joy, etc., seek Him. He loves when we reach out to Him. I want you to understand that GOD LOVES YOU!

HAVE YOU SEEN *OUR* FATHER?

So you shall serve The Lord your God, and He will bless your bread and your water. And I will take sickness away from the midst of you. -Exodus 23:25

O Lord my God, I cried out to you, and You healed me. -Psalm 30:2

The Lord will strengthen him on his bed of illness. -Psalm 41:3

Fear not, for I am with you; Be not dismayed, for I am your God. I will strengthen you, Yes I will help you, I will uphold you with My righteous right hand. -Isaiah 41:10

The Lord shall preserve you from all evil; He shall preserve your soul. -Psalm 121:7

Indeed the wages of the laborer who mowed your fields, which you kept back by fraud, cry out; and the cries of the reapers have reached the ears of The Lord of Sabaoth. -James 5:4

There are many plans in a man's heart, Nevertheless the Lords counsel — that will stand. -Psalm 19:21

For I know the thoughts that I think towards you, say The Lord, thoughts of peace and not of evil, to give you a future and a hope.
-Jeremiah 29:11

2

SKYSCRAPERS

Have you ever stood before a skyscraper and attempted to look up to the very top? I personally experienced this once in downtown Manhattan, NYC. While observing some of the largest skyscrapers in the world, I nearly broke my neck attempting to see the peaks of some buildings. As I leaned backward, I began to think and reflect on life. I wondered who in their right mind would ever clean those windows? A person like me couldn't fathom just being up that high and hanging off side of one of those tall buildings, let alone executing a task while I was up there. The fact that anyone could do this job simply amazed me. Somewhere out there, there are people who are brave enough to do this job. They work hard week in and week out. The more I thought about their occupation, the more I thought that these people were absolutely insane. Who in their right mind would trust a couple of cables to secure his life?

Thinking about this occupation left me baffled. Well, until the moment I realized the correlation between myself and the window cleaner. In actuality the window cleaner and I truly aren't so different from each other. In the same way that I thought he was crazy for trusting a cable with his life, many people think I'm crazy for having faith in Jesus Christ. Some people think that I am absolutely insane for trusting God with my life. Like the window cleaner, I am not afraid to place my life in the hands of a greater force. I am confident that if I ever slip and fall, my greater force will surely save me.

In life, we Christians are much like the high rise window cleaner. We are seen as crazy people by the outside world. The outside world observes us with skepticism: "What if the guy falls or drops his equipment? What if God directs you Christians the wrong way and doesn't save you? "These are the questions skeptics ask. But for we believers, our faith far outweighs the questioning.

The window washer and the Christian both have faith in what they are doing. In life I have learned that many people fear what they do not understand. For instance, people who clean these windows must take part in strenuous training. In this training they learn all of the nuances of the occupation. They learn the various safety precautions, proper methods, and different techniques. It is that training that gives them the confidence to hang outside a window that is forty or fifty stories high. Similarly, as Christians we go through our own version of training. Through the word of God we learn how to correctly do our jobs. In essence, we are the high rise window cleaners hired by a cleaning service company. Some of us have been in this profession for years and others are new to the field.

Remember when we first began this job? Let's flash back. Some of us were quite nervous and uncertain about our career choice. The night prior we thought about many "what if" scenarios: What if I don't do a good job? What if I am not secured by the cable? Like many people who are on the brink of becoming born again, the moment before you take the plunge is when you worry the most. At this moment some of us find ourselves asking questions similar to those the cleaner asked. What if I screw up or sin? Truth is, I can promise that you will do both. You will screw up and you will sin. No cleaner in this company will do a perfect job. However, we all should aim and attempt to be perfect. With diligent work, everyone can become a better employee.

> *For all have sinned and fall short of the glory*
> *of God. -Romans 3:23*

It takes time and experience to work toward perfecting our craft. Along the journey there will be a lot of trial and error. What's important about this process is how you respond to those errors and mistakes. Are you going to let it stop you and your practices? It wouldn't be practical to quit. You should learn from your mistakes and work toward not repeating the same ones. From that point forward, focus on becoming a better you. Our God is patient and knows that we will make mistakes. But, like the cleaner's boss, our Lord wants us to learn from our mistakes. Through this lesson He wants us to put effort into improving.

> *Neither do I condemn you; go and sin no more. -John 8:11*

There are many people who look at our profession with fear and doubt. As workers for the Lord's company, any doubt or fear that we have must leave. There's no way we can do this profession without having faith in the cable that holds us. The same is true for us as Christians; we can't be in the Kingdom and doubt the power of God. Have faith that God will guide and shield you.

> *So Jesus answered and said to them, "Have faith in God.*

For assuredly, I say to you, whoever says this mountain, Be removed and be cast into the sea, and does not doubt in his heart, but believes that those things he says will be done, he will have whatever he says.

Therefore I say to you whatever things you ask for when you pray, believe that you receive them, and you will have them." -Mark 11:22-24

The work shift begins at the service headquarters around eight p.m. After he clocks in, the cleaner takes a look at the schedule board and notices that he's scheduled nights and weekends only. Out of curiosity he asks his boss why he was scheduled for these shifts. The boss explains that by working those hours, interruptions, distractions, and errors will be minimized. During the day there are many things that can affect the proficiency of the worker. One of the greatest factors would be other people. During the day, the area is much more congested with people inside the building and down below on the street. With so many people present, sometimes there are distractions and interruptions. So, by avoiding that time period the worker can give his undivided attention to the task at hand. This is kind of like followers of Christ. It appears that God shines the brightest during our darkest moments (night shift) and when no one is around. Even though

He is always with us, we sometimes hear His voice a bit louder when we are in trouble. Sometimes God will use this isolated dark moment as a time for Him to communicate with us. Sometimes in life we are surrounded by people or things that aren't necessarily right for us. When we are in these situations, God's voice can seem distorted because of the distractions around us. An example of this can be shown in Genesis with Joseph. In Genesis, Joseph served as the King's favorite servant. He was prized and treated better than other servants. But then Joseph was forced to go through a dark time and was falsely accused of a crime for which he was imprisoned. While in prison, he was able to clearly listen to God's voice. By being able to hear God's voice he acquired a gift that got him out of prison. Not only did it get him out of prison, it put him in the prestigious position of Governor.

The cleaner arrives to the first skyscraper, which happens to be the tallest in the city. He and a partner set up the anchor at the roof of the building. The cleaner is then strapped into a harness with two security lines. The cleaner feels perfectly safe once he's locked in. What gives him comfort is the knowledge that the cable that supports him can hold up to 10,000 pounds. His knowledge about the cables is what creates his faith. As followers of God we have knowledge of His strength and capabilities. From here, faith is developed. The cleaner gains his knowledge through training, just like followers of Christ. We get our training by reading the Bible, taking part in fellowship, and practicing what we learn.

> *But grow in the grace and knowledge of our Lord and Savior Jesus Christ. To Him be the glory both now and forever. Amen. -2 Peter 3:18*

> *Not forsaking the assembling of ourselves together, as is the manner of some, but exhorting one another, and so much the more as you see the Day approaching -Hebrews 10:25*

> *Therefore comfort each other and edify one another, just as you also are doing -1 Thessalonians 5:11*

Right now the cleaner stands at the top of the building in comfort. He knows momentarily he'll have to step down and fulfill a task. At this very moment we will find out just how much faith he has in the cable. Here is where reality really sets in. As a cleaner you can read about the job all you want and speak to coworkers about it all day long, but if you don't physically do the job, what's the use of speaking about it?

> *What does it profit, my brethren, if someone says he has faith but does not have works? Can faith save him? -James 2:14*

As children of God, the same thing applies to us. We can read our Bible every day of our lives. We can meet and preach the gospel with other Christians all we want. If we don't apply what we learn and exercise our faith, however, what kind of job are we really doing as Christians? I know that sometimes taking that leap of faith and stepping off the side of the building can be intimidating. But we must trust God. He has work for us to do, so there's no way that He'll set us up for failure. Across the world there are many people being called by God to step off of the building and clean the window. There are people thinking about quitting their jobs to chase their dreams. If you're being led by God, He is saying, "Take that leap of faith, I won't let you go." There are people thinking about leaving unhealthy relationships. If you're being led by God, He is saying, "Take that leap of faith, I won't let you go." There are people thinking about packing up and moving to cities where no one knows them. Again if you are being led by God, He is saying to you, "Take that leap of faith, I won't let you go." There are some people in church afraid to tithe their ten percent because they are struggling financially to pay their bills. God is saying, "Have faith and take the leap of faith! I won't let you go; I will take care of your debt." Honestly the list goes on. Is it tough to take this leap of faith? Yes, it can be! At times it can be uncomfortable, but you must be faithful to The Lord. During this discomfort there is only one thing you can do and that is to turn to God. Just pray to Him and have faith. You can either pray or you can worry, but you can't do both. The moment you worry after prayer, you're showing that you don't believe God will deliver you.

So the cleaner decides to step down onto the side of the building. He feels comfortable as he approaches his first window. He glances down, but doesn't experience any fear because he knows that the cable won't fail him. He looks down a second time and his concern arises. He asks his coworker, who is at the top of the building, "Hey, what happens if I accidentally drop the brush or the window fluid?" His coworker says, "Don't worry, both the cleaner and the brush are strapped to you as well. We are also covered through insurance."

The brush and the window fluid are symbolic of the principles and qualities that we gain once we step into the Kingdom. When we step into the Kingdom, as long as we stay disciplined in the word of God, we will never lose our principles or qualities. Like the brush and fluid, those traits are strapped to us as well. By this I mean everything that we gained spiritually will always be attached to us. This is because the Holy Spirit resides in us. Even when we slip up or lose our grip, God will always find a way to reach us. Through the Holy Spirit, our Lord will always be able to reach us. The greatest example of this is found in prisons across the world. There are many great people who are locked up. Some of these people are God's children who just experienced a lapse of judgment. While they were cleaning their windows they happened to lose their grip on their cleaning supplies. Notice how their security cable (God) is still holding on to them firmly? So firmly that they can still reach back down to their supplies and pick up where they left off. So if you happen to be in prison reading this, just know that God hasn't given up on you. So don't you dare give up on Him. He is currently holding you up because there is still work to be done. These windows (life) are filthy with salt, residue, dust, water-stains, and pollen (past mistakes). No matter how dirty your windows are, there is still time to clean them. Just pick up your cleaning supplies, which remain attached to you through the Holy Spirit. I know some people are reading this and saying, "Hey, this is easier said than done." Honestly you may be right; however, I am speaking the truth. I know the window in front of you appears to be filthy, but you must look past it. Look past the filth and don't accept it. Don't look at this task as impossible. It's not impossible, and don't forget about the person whose office is on the other side of that window. That filth that is front of you is affecting their view as well. You're not just cleaning your window for yourself; there are other people counting on you. This ultimately means that the mistakes you have made have altered many lives around you. Since God (your cable) is still holding you up, that means that you still have the opportunity to make a change – a change that not only helps your life, but also the lives of the people who are counting on you. As long as God is with you, you can still make corrections to your life. There will be no one who can change that (Romans 8:31).

So the window cleaner picks up his brush and cleaning fluid. He proceeds to wipe the window, ultimately cleaning away the filth and dirt. The window is now perfectly clear, thanks to the diligence and perseverance of the window cleaner.

> *If God is for us who can be against us?*
> *-Romans 8:31*

3

WE THE CHILDREN

I n the Bible we are referred to as "Children of God." In actuality we are just that. We are God, The Father's children. Think about it: before we were even born God loved us unconditionally. He doesn't want us hanging around the wrong crowds. There are moments when we may notice that he warns us about certain people (Proverbs 23:9). Our Father is very protective of us. He never wants anything bad to happen to us. He will also absolutely destroy any force that may attack or bother His children (Psalm 121:7). Like many parents, He has a vision for the lives of His children and wants them to live up to their full potentials (Jeremiah 29:11). Yet, He knows we will not be perfect. He knows that there will be times when we make mistakes (Romans 3:23). Even though it hurts Him when we screw up, He still loves us nevertheless. He will always be there for us. The Father admires us and gets excited whenever we make progress. When we first turn our head toward God's Kingdom, The Father is there smiling. He is also there to encourage you to keep progressing. From there we begin to crawl into the Kingdom. The Father remains infatuated with us and encourages us to keep crawling toward Him. Next we are encouraged to take the next natural step which is walking in the Kingdom. At this very moment we may be a little nervous and quite unsure about our next steps. Don't be alarmed as this is fairly common. As humans, moving around uncharted territory can be very nerve-wracking. Don't let the nerves prevent you from progressing to the next level. The best part of traveling this route is that you don't have to face these challenges alone. We have the All-Time best dad. What we will notice is that our Heavenly Father holds our hand as we learn to walk. He is there every step of the way to guide us. From this we will see our confidence begin to grow and our nerves begin to disappear. As He holds our hands, we begin to enthusiastically take steps. We then begin to repetitively practice our steps. At this moment our Father will test us to see if we are ready to move on to the next level. And here is where we notice that he may let go of our hands to see if we can walk independently. As we stand in the center of His Kingdom, He helps, guides, and encourages us to walk toward Him on our own. As we begin to take our steps He stands in front of us with his arms wide open. He reaches out to us, cheering us on the entire time. As we begin to take our steps toward Him, the more excited He becomes. If we shall ever fall in this process, He is always there to pick us back up. He stands us back up and set us up to walk again. As our Father, He understands that while we learn to walk in the Kingdom, we may take some wrong steps. There are times when we will fall down. Sometimes when we fall down it may hurt and we might even cry. But our Father loves us so much that He'll always be there to lift us. Whenever we cry out to Him, He's always there to come to our rescue.

> *Do not speak in the hearing of a fool. For he will despise the wisdom of your words.*
> *-Proverbs 23:9*

> *The Lord shall preserve you from all evil; He shall preserve your soul. —Psalm 121:7*

> *For I know my thoughts that I think towards you, says The Lord, thoughts of peace and not of evil, to give you a future and a hope.*
> *-Jeremiah 29-11*

> *For all have sinned and fall short of the glory of God. -Romans 3:23*

During our toddler stage of spirituality, we are still curious about the world and everything in it. We see flashy things and are drawn to them. At this point we are known to make messes with our lives and throw tantrums. When we make our messes, our Father will yell to us to try to prevent us from making the mistake. At those times, some of us are disobedient and ignore our Father's instruction. Here is the point where we disappoint our Father. He warns us not to do these things because He knows the mess that they will cause. There comes a point in these situations where God has to discipline us. He could allow us to continue to make mistakes, but He loves us too much. There are times when He has to put us in timeout. He doesn't do this because He wants to, but because he wants us to reflect on our mistakes. When we are being disciplined we may absolutely hate it and may lack understanding. For the time being we may not understand; however, when we grow up spiritually we will understand. Once we gain that understanding we should thank our Father for His actions. In truth, even when we do not understand, we should still thank Him. There are also scenarios where He may discipline us as a way to slow us down. In those timeout moments, God is able to work on us. Through this disciplinary action we are able to speak to our Father and see what we did wrong. After timeout is over we must learn from our mistake and not do it again (Acts 3:19). As we grow spiritually, life very well may become more complex. How can our Father trust us with greater responsibilities when we're still screwing up small responsibilities?

Growing spiritually with our Heavenly Father is just like any other parent-child relationship. Except it's actually greater! Through our actions as children we may go through three different phases. These phases consist of adolescent, teenage, and adult phases. Each phase symbolizes a different level of spiritual maturity. As followers we all aim to reach the adult stage of spirituality. Reaching this is quite challenging but we can all achieve it.

> *Repent therefore and be converted, that your sins may be blotted out, so that times of refreshing may come from the presence of the Lord. -Acts 3:19*

Adolescent

At this stage in our spirituality some of us are knowledgeable of who our Heavenly Father is and have developed a genuine love for Him. In this stage we are completely dependent on our parent. This is absolutely all right because our parent wants to see us grow. He doesn't want to miss any steps that we take. Sometimes when we are in this stage, we develop a "give me" mentality. We feel a sense of entitlement and we believe that things are ours, when in actuality they belong to our Heavenly Father. This is fairly common with children when their parent gives them an interesting item to hold. Sometimes the item is flashy, lights up, and looks very exciting. The parent gives it to the child because of the joy it brings to the child. So immediately the child grabs the item and stakes their claim on it. Eventually the time comes where the parent takes the item back. That is when the child throws a tantrum, screams, cries, and yells "It's mine!!!" The child thinks the item is theirs, as if they got the item on their own. Does this sound familiar? In life we humans do the same thing with our Heavenly Father. We begin to make claims on things that our Heavenly Father gave us. God gave us these things because He loves to see us joyful. So what are these items?

These items can be many things such as money, jobs, relationships, material items, talent, etc. Let's understand that none of these items truly belong to us. They belong to our Father. One of the most common items that we try to claim is money. Some people let money control their lives and also their better judgment. With this money evil is brought and people develop selfish and greedy tendencies. They claim the money as being "theirs." This is especially evident when followers of Christ attend church. In every church service there comes a time for tithing. In some instances, when the collection plate is being passed, people tense up and clinch their wallets. They may look at their cash and have a strong debate about what to tithe. If a person received $100 dollars on their paycheck, the correct amount to tithe is at least $10. In the word of God it says that He wants our first and best 10 percent (Proverbs 3:9). Sometimes when we have the adolescent spiritual mindset we lose sight of the word of God. From this we develop preposterous theories like, "They only want my money so that they can pocket it." As children of God we must acknowledge that we are tithing to honor our relationship with God. Now, it's true that there may very well be corrupt churches and pastors, but we must let God deal with those issues. We are not tithing for them. When we tithe, we should understand that as a children of God, the money in our pockets is not our own. The money belongs to our Heavenly Father. He lets us hold the shiny item because He wants to bring joy to us. So in this time let's understand that items we treasure truly belong to our parent. This parent is letting us borrow it for the moment. Honestly, for quite some time I battled with this concept myself. Let's say I made $100 from work that week. I would be in church and I would dread the passing of the collection plate. I would look in my wallet noticing that I had only two single dollar bills, some 10s and 20s. In my head I would think, *Well I'm definitely not giving the church a 10 or 20...they are just going to pocket it...I could actually use the 10s and 20s for something...so I'll just give them this two dollars and they can do what they want with it.* It took leaving my job for me to realize just how petty I was being with money that truly didn't belong to me. For instance, if God never blessed me with that job, I would have never received that $100 to begin with. My second mistake with tithing was feeling obligated because of the perception I felt I was giving to others. I didn't want people to look at me differently and judge me. From this I learned not to worry about what anyone else thought about my tithing, but only to worry about what The Lord thought. After all, by tithing I was showing my gratitude to The Lord for all that He had done in my life. I am also taking away any stronghold that the money might have over me or my life. By sharing my first and best with God, I was showing that I place nothing above Him. Think about it: there are more than 200 million unemployed people in the world today. Why am I so special that I am not one of them? The answer is that I'm not that special. God's grace is what made me special enough to have that job, which made that money. I didn't understand that until the conditions at my job became unbearable. At that point I felt as if I had to quit my job. Right then I became just another statistic – a part of those 200 million unemployed individuals. I know that in my life God has shown me so much undeserved love and grace. Sometimes we get so used to our comfy situations that we begin to take them for granted. We also may not acknowledge the fact that it is God who is working in our lives. We get so used to God's grace that we begin to feel entitled to His blessing of money. Let's humble ourselves and gain an understanding that God owes us absolutely nothing. We owe Him!!! We have a debt to Him that can never be paid off. There is no possession that we can accumulate that can pay for the blood of Christ on the cross. With that understanding, let's analyze what God is truly asking for. He is *only* asking for our first and best 10 percent (Leviticus 23:12). Yes, that is it! So after coming to that realization I made a vow to give God my first and best 10 percent. The word of God says that not only will He take the 10 percent, He will protect it, bless the remaining 90 percent, and give it back in abundance. An example of this is shown in Genesis with Cain and Abel. Abel gave God his first and best. In return God blessed him and Abel received great favor. Meanwhile Cain gave to The Lord, but it certainly wasn't His best. In return he received the opposite of Abel's favor.

On a lasting note, the giving of 10 percent doesn't only apply to financial income. It really applies to almost every aspect of life, even to something as simple as how you spend your day. Set aside some quality time for God. A great time to do this is first thing in the morning. As soon as you wake up, pray, read the word of God, and meditate. Spend quality time with your Heavenly Father. From there watch how he blesses the rest of your day.

> *Bring all the tithes into the storehouse, That there may be food in My house, And try Me now in this," Says the Lord of hosts, "If I will not open for you the windows of Heaven And pour out for you such blessing That there will not be room enough to receive it And I will rebuke the devourer for your sakes, So that*

he will not destroy the fruit of your ground.
-Malachi 3:10-11

Another flashy item that our parent gives us and that we like to claim as our own is relationships. As humans we sometimes don't like to acknowledge that God places certain people in our lives for a reason. These relationships could be developed with significant others, family members, or friends. Believe it or not, we didn't form these relationships on our own. Sometimes in our relationships we lose sight of this. We can be in a great relationship with someone and ultimately take them for granted. We can get so used to our significant others doing so much for us that we grow accustomed to the great things. When that happens, we lose sight that the favors these people show us are actually complete blessings from God. Sometimes we can be in the darkest moments of our lives and still feel entitled to whatever that person has provided us. Let's take a second to look at ourselves in the mirror. We may be in a place in life where we cannot offer them anything. Let's be honest. No, our "good looks" do not equate to the favor we're shown. No, our "great jokes" do not equate to the favor we are shown. No, "who we used to be" does not equate to the favor we are shown. Some of us have absolutely nothing and have people who completely provide for us. Then we choose to mistreat them as if our looks, personality, or status gives us license to do this. First let's acknowledge that every last one of those traits were given by God and can be taken at any moment. Not to mention that God placed those people in your life for a reason. No, you are not entitled to these relationships. Don't take for granted the relationships God has blessed you with. These people are a gift from God that you do not deserve. Show your appreciation for these gifts by treating them right. Some of us are unemployed and have people who help us out financially. Some of us have been abandoned by everyone we ever loved. Yet God has blessed us with people to vent to who are trustworthy. Some of us physically can't do anything by ourselves. Somehow God sent you a person to compensate for your lack of ability. When you disrespect or abuse these people, not only are you doing it to them, but you are doing it to God as well. You are like the child throwing those toys back at your parent. You are telling your parent that these gifts are not good enough. Sadly enough, some of us don't realize that some relationships are gifts until we lose them.

The next set of items that our parent gives us that we like to take claim over is material items. Some of us have been blessed enough to acquire great material wealth like luxurious cars and designer clothing. Some of us acquire these items and think that we acquired them on our own. "Well I worked hard to get here." This may be true, but also notice that God put you in position to work hard so you could, in fact, acquire these items. Some of us believe that because we are in a higher tax bracket we are better than other people.

Some of us believe that because of the jewelry or designer clothes we wear, we shouldn't socialize with people who have less – as if those people are not good enough to be in our presence. Do not get so attached to your material items that you lose sight of what's important in life, which is living right by God. There is one thing in life no one can ever avoid and that is death. When we die, we will not be able to take anything with us. Every last one of us will have to stand before God and account for our lives. I highly doubt that you can live an evil life, disrespect God, refuse to repent, and still get into Heaven based on your designer shoes. Do you really think that God will stand there and say, "Well you did all of these evil things, worshipped everything but me, and denied me...however, I do love those designer shoes. Where did you get them...hmm I'll make an exception for you, welcome to Heaven." Seriously! These material things are a form of the idols that God warns us not to worship. This is demonstrated in both the Old and New Testament. Don't let these items take control of your life. These items are not yours. God has blessed you and made it possible for you to acquire or keep these items.

One of the final items that our parent lets us hold that we claim as our own is our gifts of talent. By that I mean athletic abilities, singing, leadership, and so forth. There are so many gifts that God gives us – the key words being, *gives us*. God gives us these gifts so that we can share them with others in His name.

Sometimes these gifts allow us to live a life in luxury and with a great abundance of favor. Sometimes we bask too much in the glory that comes with these gifts. From this glory, if we are not grounded and humble, we gain a sense of arrogance. Yes, our gift has led us to fame and a life of luxury, and sometimes we can be forgetful of how we acquired this gift. Sometimes these gifted people use their fame as an excuse to look down on others. Just because others admire your gift and place you on a pedestal, don't let it go to your head. The fame that you acquired came from a gift, which came from God. No, you didn't get this gift on your own. Think about it: what do you think will happen when you can no longer perform your sport at such a high level? What will happen when you can no longer hit those high notes when performing? Do you think that people will still follow you and chant your name? The large number of people who flock to you because of your talents do so just for your talents. Their loyalty is attached to your gifted talents, not to you as a person. Without your gift, these people and/or fans will not be around. Understand what a blessing this gift is in your life and give credit where it's due. These people are attached to the gift that comes from God. Thus, if you stay attached to God, you may have grace with all of the glory that comes with your gift. That is unless God's will says differently.

After observing all of the items that The Lord gives us, we should realize that we are not entitled to anything. The things that we children claim as our own cause us to have unnecessary attachments. Why are we so attached to the item that our parent has given us? Why do we throw tantrums and yell, "It's mine," when actually we, as the adolescent, have absolutely nothing. We are solely dependent on The Lord for everything. So, no, these items aren't ours. They belong to our Heavenly Father who has blessed us with the opportunity to hold them. So don't become attached to the item. Instead, become attached to The Lord. We must decide if we are going to live by the item, or live by God. We cannot do both. The word of God says that we cannot worship two masters. That means we must decide to either worship God or these other idols. Without God we are nothing and we are no one.

No one can serve two masters; for either he will hate the one and love the other, or else he will be loyal to the one and despise the other. You cannot serve God and mammon. -Matthew 6:24

I am the vine, you are the branches. He who abides in Me and I in him, bears much fruit; for without Me you can do nothing. -John 15:5

Teenage

Another stage of spiritual maturity that we may experience is the teenage phase. At this stage of spiritually we go through a lot of changes in our spiritual body. At times we may be afraid of these changes and feel as if we are alone. Little do we know that our parent understands the changes we are experiencing. Instead of pushing them away, we should seek our parent for guidance. Sometimes while going through these spiritual changes we feel unsure about ourselves. We also believe our parents are incapable of relating to us. We are going through changes that are definitely noticeable. We feel uncomfortable because we haven't become acclimated to them yet. This initial discomfort is normal and yes, you do appear different to others, but stay strong. In real life teenagers go through these changes as well; their bodies and voices change, they blossom, etc. In the spiritual realm we teenagers also go through noticeable changes. We may not take part in the same things that we used to. We may begin to speak differently. We may also change our priorities. The great Bishop TD Jakes said it best: "You can't be who you're going to be and who you used to be at the same time."

In this stage you may very well be teased about your changes by other teenagers. The teenagers who do the teasing will be the teenagers of the world. The teenagers of the Kingdom will not tease you for your changes because they understand and can relate to you. The teenagers of the world may ridicule you because of your changes. Don't let their words get to you. Stay firm in your faith. Another interesting thing about the teenage stage of spirituality is the way we rebel. At this stage, our self-discipline isn't where our Heavenly Father would like it to be. So there are instances when we ignore instruction and feel we can take matters into our own hands. As teenagers, we like to ignore the rules and instructions of our parents, and by doing that, we fail to see that our parent is giving us rules for our own good. So there may very well be times where our parent has to discipline us or punish us for our disobedience. He may very well be saying to you, "I'm punishing you for this specific reason... You will understand when you grow up." Once we grow in our spirituality we will reflect back and understand why certain things happened. So at this stage we must understand that in the outside world there are forces that will tempt us to disobey our Heavenly Father. Sometimes when we are in the Kingdom we may do something that we know is absolutely wrong. At those times we let our curiosity get the best of us.

I know this is a tough time because you are going through changes, but our Heavenly Father wants us to make a decision. Are we going to live within the rules of the household (Kingdom) or are we going to live like the rest of the world? We can't do both. While we live under The Lord's roof, we'd better abide by his rules.

> *So then because you are lukewarm, and neither cold nor hot, I will vomit you out of My mouth. -Revelation 3:16*

So which side are we on? We cannot be who we used to be and who we are going to be at the same time. Nevertheless, our Father understands that we are sinners and that we will make mistakes. But He wants us to seek Him when we make mistakes. He wants us to seek Him so He can help us fix our problems. Sometimes as teenagers we try to fix our problems on our own. We mistakenly think we can hide our wrong doings from our parents (as if we can really get away with lying to our parents). Understand that we all make mistakes; just go to our Heavenly Father and confess and repent. From there allow him to fix things. When we try to fix things on our own, we just make things worse. There is no way we can hide or lie to the Father. An example of this is shown in Genesis after Adam and Eve ate the fruit and covered their private parts with branches. They covered their bodies when they weren't supposed to know that they were naked. The only way that they could have known such information was by having eaten from the tree. After trying to cover up their shame, they were caught and disciplined. Sometimes when we make our mistakes, it's possible that we may also be disciplined. From this discipline God wants us to learn our lesson. For instance, sometimes when you are doing the wrong thing, God may do something to make you slow down and change your pace. This change of pace could involve prison, health issues, etc. When we are in this slowed down state we are able to see who really has our best interest. In this state, the things we once desired of the world abandon us. Worldly things like money, greed, addictions, etc., cannot restore your life. So when you're down and out, where is the world to be found? The only one who truly cares and can enrich your life when you are in this state is God.

Adult

At this stage of spirituality we understand our parent a lot more. We begin to view our parent as not only an authority figure but as a friend as well. We understand the disciplinary actions that we were given at a younger age. We are more comfortable speaking with our parent now than we have ever been. Something that we should be careful about when we are adults is not to go spiritually astray from our parent. Keep seeking our Heavenly Father for guidance. We might look back at how far we've come, and how much knowledge and wisdom we have acquired and begin to feel as if we know it all. This will cause us to react to situations in a fleshly manner. We must understand that we can never know it all. No matter how good we are as Christians, there is still work to be done and we can always be better. Don't get complacent; continue to work hard for The Lord. It's like being a great athlete; we can always be better. We can never be the greatest child in God's Kingdom. No one will ever come close to Jesus' greatness. But even though we will never reach Jesus' greatness, we can focus on becoming a better us. Adopt the

Michael Jordan mentality for the Kingdom of God. By this I mean focus on always being a better you. There was a point when professional basketball player Michael Jordan was at the top of his career. But even when he was viewed as the best, he wasn't complacent. He kept challenging himself to get better in different areas. One year he may have focused on three-point shots and mastered then. Then he focused on defense, and mastered it, and so forth. He was relentless and kept pushing himself. So for us, we may have executed the concept of patience. So now let's focus on obedience. Then execute that. All in all, keep trying to be the best you can be for The Lord. By doing this, you not only make God happy, you also help the Kingdom grow and strengthen. The children of God who make it to the adult stage of spirituality should view themselves as blessed. We must understand that there's a lot of responsibility that comes with being an adult. We are now the leaders and role models for people who are growing up spiritually. We are also leaders and role models for those who have yet to join the Kingdom. You may not notice it, but there are a lot of people watching your moves. Some of these people look up to you and want to emulate you. Don't be the person who misleads them. It's important to put your best foot forward. Give your best effort because you are a representation of the Heavenly Father for the rest of the world. Take pride in the Kingdom to which you belong. Let's make our Heavenly Father proud of us.

4

THE ROAD TRIP

Sometimes in life we receive a message from The Lord that might not seem as if it makes complete sense to us. As humans we can be so prideful and think that we always know what's best. As children of God we must learn to humble ourselves and just flat out trust God.

> *Therefore humble yourselves under the mighty hand of God, that He may exalt you in due time. -1 Peter 5:6*

> *God resist the proud, but gives grace to the humble. -James 4:6*

I mean, seriously, how can we even compare to His greatness? The answer is simple! WE CAN'T!!! Our Heavenly Father created the entire universe in six days.

What's crazy about that is he still had a day to spare for rest. How much pride could one person have to think that we could possibly know better? Fact of the matter is that most of us know that God's Will is the only way. Even so, we are sometimes reluctant to try his way because it may feel uncomfortable. To us it may seem as if it doesn't make sense. As followers of Christ, we must constantly remind ourselves how tiny we are in comparison to The Lord. Honestly, his mindset/ideas are more than a trillion moves ahead of ours. It's like we're playing checkers and He's playing an unbelievably fast paced round of chess. He has seen our current moves long before we were born. He also knows where our futures are headed and knows where they end. Let's understand that He has not only seen the Promised Land, he has created it. God is the only one who has the exact directions for getting to the Promised Land.

> *Before I formed you in the womb I knew you; Before you were born I sanctified you; I ordained you a prophet to the nations.*
> *-Jeremiah 1:5*

We must therefore trust in The Lord when we don't quite understand. He knows the steps we must take, and He wants us to get to the Promised Land. In life, we humans find ourselves in many rough patches. While going through these rough patches we tend to distance ourselves away from everyone. We instantly assume that no one can relate, understand, or would approve. Once we are in this mindset, we foolishly take things into our own hands. Sometimes the hole that we've dug for ourselves obstructs our view and we fail to see who truly cares for us. This distorted vision causes false assumptions. We begin to feel that there is no one who can get us out of this hole. At this point it's fairly common for us to reach for solutions through works of the flesh, ultimately leaving us to forget about the one clear cut, guaranteed solution –seeking help from The Lord. The reason people hesitate to reach out to Him is because they feel that He won't be forgiving. They feel that what they've done is so bad He can't forgive them. They feel that because the problem derived from the flesh, they should respond in a fleshly manner. Let's settle this once and for all. This mindset is ludicrous. Erase these thoughts from your mind and never let them return. You should gain an understanding for who our God is and His traits. He is loving, generous, patient, caring, and, most important, **forgiving**. He hates to see us hurting or lost.

> *8. The Lord is merciful and gracious, slow to anger, and abounding in mercy. 9. He will not always strive with us, Nor will He keep His anger forever 10. He has not dealt with us according to our sins, Nor punished us according to our sins, Nor punished us according to our iniquities. 11. For as the*

> *heavens are high above the earth, So great*
> *is His mercy toward those who fear Him; 12.*
> *As far as the east is from the west, So far has*
> *He removed our transgressions from us. 13.*
> *As a father pities his children, So The Lord*
> *pities those who fear Him. 14. For He knows*
> *our frame; He remembers that we are dust.*
> *-Psalm 103:8-14*

In fact, if you come to Him with a sincere heart, He will make right of all your wrongs. Look at some of the most prominent Men in the Bible who committed critical sins. They sincerely sought God's forgiveness and received it. God made right their wrongs and used these men in big ways. For example, after being an adulterer, murderer, and liar, David was made King. He then converted many sinners back to the Kingdom of God. And there is Moses who killed an Egyptian Man and was still able to lead the Jews out of slavery. Honestly, this list goes on with the Apostle Paul, Peter, and others. Through these stories we learn just how forgiving and loving God truly is. Something that these men had in common is that they sincerely sought God after trouble.

All of these biblical people dug themselves into deep holes. God not only delivered them, He utilized them in tremendous ways. Just like these well-known figures, if we seek The Lord, our lives will only get better. We will witness the restoration of which He is capable. Sometimes we are too hard-headed for our own good. Luckily we belong to the greatest Kingdom to ever exist. Our Lord loves us so much and He just wants us to live great lives. Because we belong to the Kingdom, the Trinity will never leave us, even during our darkest moments.

> *For He Himself has said, I will never leave you, nor forsake you. -Hebrews 13:5*

Before stepping into the Kingdom of God, it's as if we're on a road trip with Jesus and we are the drivers. The road trip begins at night because we are all born into darkness. Darkness symbolizes that we are born into sin.

> *Behold, I was brought forth in iniquity; and in sin my mother conceived me. -Psalm 51:5*

> *For you were once darkness, but now you are light in the Lord. Live as children of light. -Ephesians 5:8*

It's said that the two most important days in a person's life are the day they were born and the day they figure out *why* they were born. Once you figure out why you were born, your life begins to make sense. The anointing that is placed on your life will take you to a place of ultimate happiness. At this point of happiness you are said to be living the life of your dreams. Some call it the American dream or the Dream life. What's amazing about this dream place is that it can be a reality for everyone. What's even better about this dream place is that God actually wants us to have it. The only way we can get there, though, is by following "God's word." Many people miss out on this dream life because they go astray from The Lord. They then think that their dream life is just that, a dream. This dream is only obtainable to those who are willing to open their eyes and wake up. Please note that each of us has a different dream destination. A dream destination doesn't always mean a life of luxury or fame. The place lies with your anointing and gives you a sense of completeness. There was a point in my life when I was extremely obsessed with money. I thought that if I received large amounts of money my life would have a sense of completeness. Boy was I wrong. My entire mindset changed when The Lord spoke to me during meditation. I was in college and had the most money that I'd ever had. It was $2,000. To some this isn't much. But to a young man who didn't grow up with a silver spoon, this was plenty. With this money I bought the latest music technology, jewelry, and clothes. Honestly, for that "first week" I felt like I was the king of the world. I would parade around with my latest purchase in front of the mirror. Notice how I said the "first week." After that I felt an emptiness because I still had to live in reality.

How could I possibly have peace of mind when everyone in my life was still struggling? At that very moment I realized that the joy the money brought me had an expiration date. So I went through a period of time afterward where I felt very down. I wasn't sure who I was. My back was against the wall. I ran out of ideas about how to maintain happiness. One day I sat in my room alone and turned off all the distractions around me such as my cell phone, television, radio, computer, etc. I sat there looking at the ceiling. I got into a mental place where God and I could talk one-on-one. In this conversation I asked God why I felt so down and borderline depressed. I asked him why the money and my achievements hadn't brought me happiness. His response was simple. He told me, "These rewards weren't from me." He then told me, and I quote, "The paradise that you envisioned when you had the money cannot be obtained here on earth. That paradise you envisioned only exists in Heaven with Me. So focus on living through My word and one day you will rejoice in the real paradise." From that very moment I vowed to place my life in God's hands only. From that point I realized the only way to make it to my destination was through God. As humans it can be quite challenging getting to this state of mind, but we must stop resisting. The reason it is so tough is because we're born in darkness (sin).

So, our road trip with Jesus begins very early in the morning – around 3 a.m. when it's still dark. As drivers we are initially in control of the wheel and the directions that we wish to take. As drivers, The Lord has given us free will to decide the directions we want to go in the vehicle we call life. The road trip we are on appears to be long at times; however, it actually goes by quite fast. On this one trip we drive through everything: dark times, light times, storms, and clear skies. But we all start our road trip when it's dark. At the very start, we begin by adjusting our mirrors, our seats, and becoming familiar with the vehicle. We are basically trying to find our place in the vehicle and in life. While we make our adjustments some uncertainties may arise. The only way to get past those uncertainties is to actually begin driving. So we finally hit the pedal. The entire time we're driving, God knows where our final destination is and how to get there. He wants to give us the directions, but He also wants us to reach out to Him for guidance.

> *But from there you will seek The Lord your God, and you will find Him if you search for Him with all of your heart and soul. -Deuteronomy 4:29*

> *If My people who are called by My name will humble themselves and pray and seek My face and turn from their wicked ways, then I will hear from heaven, and will forgive their sin and heal their land. -2 Chronicles 7:14*

But without faith it is impossible to please Him, for he who comes to God must believe that He is and that He is a rewarded of those who diligently seek him. -Hebrews 11:6

So we just begin driving. Do we always know where we are going? No, but we don't want our passenger to know that. Here we are driving, and we don't exactly know where we're going. So we take a couple of chances on turns. Does our passenger Jesus know when we are lost? Absolutely, but He wants us to seek Him for guidance.

Would not God find this out? For He knows the secrets of the heart. -Psalm 44-21

We turn left and there is a road block ahead. Road blocks happen all the time in life. The kinds of blocks vary depending on the person. Maybe you didn't get the promotion you wanted; maybe a loved one passed away; maybe you were diagnosed with an illness; maybe you're dealing with a difficult relationship break-up; maybe you relapsed on an addiction. Whatever the case may be, your trip shouldn't end just because there's a road block. A roadblock only means that an adjustment needs to be made. So what is the correct adjustment to get you back on track? The answer is simple: follow the word of God. The truth is that many of us are arrogant and believe that we can take things into our own hands. So we back out and do a K-Turn. God directs us to turn right, but we ignore Him. We ignore His direction because, for whatever reason, we believe that we know a better way. A way that we've convinced ourselves makes more sense. So we turn left instead. Once we turn left and drive for about five miles we encounter a treacherous storm. Storms like this in life can be a very scary time. Sometimes the storm is massive, like debt, abuse, poverty, drugs, etc. But as children of The Lord, we should remind ourselves that these storms are meant to pass. While we are driving through this storm we can't see through the windshield or in our rear view mirror. This is the moment you remember that you were instructed to turn in the other direction. Now, as you glance in your rear view mirror, you can't help regretting how things turned out. Well don't beat yourself up about it too much. It's now a thing of the past. You must know that, through Christ, this storm will pass. Not to mention that the only way to get past the storm is to go through it. That's when you become bold enough to ask, "Why did God let me do this, or allow this to happen to me?" Well honestly, He told you where to turn but you failed to listen. You decided to exercise your free will and go in the opposite direction. He's not always going to force you to go in a certain direction. But if something isn't right, he will most certainly alert you as much as possible. Sometimes how you react to the alert will determine the outcome. He wants people to follow Him who sincerely want to follow Him. Yes, He is powerful enough to make us all follow Him, but He wants people to sincerely seek Him. It's also possible that the storm you're going through is meant to mold you for the future. He could be helping you gain wisdom. Our Lord works in mysterious ways and knows how to bring out our full potential. You see, He loves you unconditionally and wants you to display your unconditional love for Him as well. This love is displayed by obeying His word and living in a manner that makes Him proud. He is our Heavenly Father and wants us to reach to Him for guidance. The moment you do this, you will be led to your correct destination. Meanwhile, when you're driving through these storms, you are left with a few options that you brainstorm.

1.) You can continue driving carelessly on the same path and at the same speed. Honestly we all know that's not good. Why? Because it leads to destruction and death! Just as in regular life. We can be going through a storm in real life and not make any adjustments. Your failure to make adjustments can lead to your demise.

2.) You might have the idea to try something that one of your friends told you about. You know, that one friend who doesn't quite have a relationship with God at all. This friend suggests that you should turn on your high beams when facing a these kinds of storms.

So you try this and drive into a railing, damaging your car and possibly yourself. Researchers say that high beams are quite bad to use when driving in harsh conditions. They cause the light to reflect back to the driver and can distort the driver's vision. What exactly are these high beams? These high beams are anything that corrupts the way you see things during a storm. Essentially they are like adopting a pessimistic mindset during a troubled time. In your current situation, this will only make things worse.

3.) You could attempt to figure things out on your own. If you do this, though, you will only be guessing. Don't forget it's still dark, it's a heavy storm, and you can't see anything. So here you are driving through the storm; which option will you select? Like many other people in your position you select the third option. You figure that because you put yourself in this predicament through acts of the flesh, that you should be the one to solve it through acts of the flesh. So you decide to turn the car right at the next intersection. Now you see that the storm gets even heavier.

4.) You still have the option of turning to God. This option is the only one that truly makes sense. For some reason, people use this as a last resort when it should actually be the first. People fail to realize that God loves us regardless, and that He has been the passenger the entire time. He actually knows the direction you should take. Now you realize that your back is against the wall. So you pray to God and he hears you. At this very moment He begins to help you. Just know that He's always working and has a plan. At this time, be patient.

> *These things I have spoken to you, that in Me you may have peace. In the world you will have tribulation; but be of good cheer; I have overcome the world. -John 16:33*

> *For I consider that the sufferings of this present time are not worthy to be compared with the glory which shall be revealed to us. -Romans 8:18*

> *I can do all things through Christ who strengthens me. -Philippians 4:13*

You finally turn to God, who is sitting next you, and you ask him to deliver you from this storm. So He leans over and flicks on your windshield wipers. Now you can see the path ahead of you a lot more clearly. You now begin to see that there is hope. His next instruction for you is to slow down a bit. Once you do, you start to notice some improvements. God then gives you a map (Bible) to refer to. So you pick it up and receive a great deal of optimism and confidence about your trip. You begin to see that your destination is still obtainable.

He tells you that if you follow His map, and learn to listen to Him while you're driving, you will reach your destination. You have to trust His word. He has seen your destination before, and knows what's in store for you. The Lord wants you to get there.

> *Before I formed you in the womb I knew you; before you were born I sanctified you; I ordained you a prophet to the nations.*
> *-Jeremiah 1:5*

Now it's five a.m. The sun hasn't quite risen, but the sky is a lot lighter than it was before. It also looks as if that the storm has calmed down to a drizzle. This is when you start feeling comfortable and complacent so you make the mistake that many people make. You decide to put your map down. You think, now that you've seen the directions there's no need to keep referring to them. You now feel as though you can handle this yourself. It appears that you have been delivered from the storm by God. So now you're extremely confident. You lean back in your chair, drive with one hand on the wheel, and blast your music. This is a mistake that some Christians make after being rescued. They become complacent with where they are, as if they have saved themselves. Never forget who delivered you from your storm. God doesn't want you to forget. He wants you to keep your map out so He can look with you and point out certain things. In this way He is able to show you the necessary steps to get to your destination. Your trip will also be easier if you humble yourself and use God's directions.

> *Therefore humble yourselves under the mighty hand of God, that He may exalt you in due time.* -1 Peter 5:6

> *God resist the proud, But gives grace to the humble.* -James 4:6

The truth is, just because God made the storm bearable doesn't mean that you should get too comfortable. Don't you ever stop reading your map (Bible) and think that you have things figured out. Keep God first at all times, listen to Him, refer to the Bible, and allow Him to work. Right now some of us are leaning back in our cars and playing our music loud, without any sense of direction. We do look cool, right? Wrong! Even when God is sitting right next to you, his voice can be distorted when you have the music blasting. We must learn to quiet down the distractions in life (loud music) and stop taking unnecessary risks (driving one-handed). We have to get in a state of mind where we can hear The Lord's instructions.

So, now you're showing arrogance and you notice that you're applying more pressure to the pedal. You're reverting back to your old ways and you are speeding. This time, because of your recklessness, your car begins to hydroplane into another car ahead of you. The storm is has gotten heavy again, making it hard to see the road. You keep driving and become scared. Here you finally start to realize that Jesus really is the only way. At this point you say the words, "Jesus take the wheel." You have tried the other ways and you've seen where they've gotten you. Now you figure it's officially time to surrender to God. So you confess to him what you did wrong and you sincerely apologize. At this very moment he welcomes you with open arms and expresses his unconditional love for you. You notice how patient and forgiving he has been with you. He truly cares for you like no other. He doesn't keep bringing up previous mistakes. Your apology, confession, and repentance are good enough for him.

> *If we confess our sins, He is faithful and just to forgive us our sins and to cleanse us from all unrighteousness. -1 John 1:9*

> *(For The Lord your God is a merciful God), He will not forsake you nor destroy you, nor forget the covenant of your fathers which He swore to them. -Deuteronomy 4:31*

You're still driving through this heavy storm and it appears that Jesus hasn't intervened quite yet. Naturally you become a little nervous. Don't be nervous. Instead, be patient. This entire time, while you disobeyed Him and rebelled, He was patient with you. Now be patient with Him. Of course He can easily deliver you out of this storm, but He wants to do it at the right time. The time will occur when you are spiritually ready to handle what your destination entails. Because of that, He may allow you to keep driving into the storm a little longer. During this extra time you will gain experience and wisdom. From this very moment you will have a testimony. You can share this testimony and help rescue someone who finds themselves in a similar storm. It is very possible that you may be the passenger on a road trip one day. Someone who's driving may need you for guidance. As followers, God lives within us all. So remember that we are supposed to be a representation of Him. It's very possible that the person you will be guiding does not know Christ. So you might be the first and last representation of what they think of Christ. For that reason, you must take pride in The Lord's word. When that time comes, God can use you as a vessel to get others out of their storms. Now that you have a testimony and experience of storms, you can adequately instruct the next person. It's always easier for a person to accept your guidance when you've actually been through it yourself.

Now you have surrendered the wheel to Jesus. Since He hasn't yet revealed His plan, you feel a little confused. You're wondering if He is going to save you again, or if you're just going to be doomed. Have faith! Little do you know that he is preparing you.

> *Because of your un-belief; for assuredly I say to you, if you have faith as a mustard seed, you will say to this mountain, "Move from here to there," and it will move; and nothing will be impossible for you. -Matthew 17:20*

While your eyes are glued on the road, you don't notice him placing your wipers on high speed. And then He lifts your leg slightly, taking pressure off the pedal, so you begin driving slower. You grip loosens and your hands are completely off of the wheel. Right then, the storm reaches its peak and up ahead you see bright light from a 16-wheeler. This symbolically illustrates the moment after you have accepted Jesus Christ's plan. You are now getting closer to your destination or anointing. Now is when the enemy will try to intervene by placing fear, doubt, or uncertainty in your mind. You look down and notice your hands are off of the wheel. The car is now going head on with the 16-wheeler. Here is the point where many people lose their way. What do you do? Grab the wheel and move out of the way or do you show faith? Are you going to trust Jesus to do what you prayed for and believe He'll take the wheel? The correct answer is to have faith and leave the wheel alone. The moment you finally accept

God's Will is when you begin to break through to your anointing.

> *And let us not grow weary while doing good,*
> *for in due time we shall reap if we do not lose*
> *heart -Galatians 6:9*

Just as the 16-wheeler begins to close in on you, Jesus grabs the wheel and turns right onto a side street. What's interesting is that the side street He turned on wasn't visible to you. On this street you notice that the sun is shining. The storm is over and you are arriving at your destination. It took a lot for you to get here. But through the grace of God you endured it and have arrived at your destination (anointing).

5

TRIP TO PARADISE

Is life beating you up? Are you tired of being in debt? Are you tired of being sick? Do you feel trapped in a bad relationship? What if I could promise you a permanent vacation away from all of those things? This vacation would be in the ultimate paradise. This place is indescribably beautiful, peaceful, and filled with nothing but love. What is this paradise that I'm speaking of?

The paradise is called Heaven. As humans, we save up our entire lives so we can afford this trip to paradise. In actuality we could truly never afford this trip. Luckily for us, our Heavenly Father controls this paradise. He gives us an unbelievably undeserved discount for this trip. We truly do not deserve this discount. This discount comes from our Lord and Savior, Jesus Christ, who paid the ultimate cost for this trip. He paid for this trip with the shedding of His blood and sacrifice. When His life was sacrificed, He gave us the opportunity to take this trip. We could never pay Him back for His contribution, but as children of God we should try our best.

This is one paradise vacation where descriptive words just can't do it any justice. There are no words that can adequately describe the beauty of this place. The brochures that we have seen do not come close to properly describing the beauty of this paradise. Everything that you read about it in the brochure (Bible) is present there. Actually seeing it, however, exceeds any vision you ever imagined. From the brochure we learned that there is no sun or moon needed to light up the location. The glory of God is what illuminates the sky. The walls are decorated with precious stones and the streets are paved with gold. This is the happiest place ever, and no one who is impure is allowed to enter. One of the most beautiful attractions is that there is no sickness, pain, or suffering, and there is no more death.

> *But as it is written: eye has not seen, nor ear heard, nor have entered into the heart of man The things which God has prepared for those who love Him. -1 Corinthians 2:9*

> *And God will wipe away every tear from their eyes; there shall be no more death, nor sorrow, nor crying. There shall be no more*

pain, for the former things have passed away.
-Revelation 21:4

What should you pack?

Okay, so we are going on the most extravagant vacation of our lives. What will we pack? When packing a bag for paradise, there are many things that we can and should bring; however, there are five essentials that we *must* bring. These five things are absolutely vital because without them this trip is not possible. You are probably wondering what these five things are.

First we must pack our *confession*. In this confession we acknowledge that Jesus Christ is Lord. This acknowledgement means that we believe that he died on the cross for our sins. We must also believe that Jesus rose again after death (Romans 10:8-9). After this confession we will be saved by God. Let it be known that God is the only one who can save us.

Second we must pack our *repentance*. At this point we should ask God to forgive us for our sins. After remorsefully asking for forgiveness, we must renew our minds. We must turn our back on sin and turn toward the Lord. Through this turning, we show God that we accept His will in our lives. This idea is illustrated in the book of John where Simon Peter failed to catch any fish. Jesus then instructed him to cast His net on the right side of the boat. The moment he did that, Peter brought in more fish than he could carry (John: 21). This symbolizes how when we finally accept God's plan, we will be tremendously blessed in abundance. Without God, those blessings are not possible.

Through the renewing of our minds we are showing God that we are truly remorseful for our sins. After our confession and repentance, we pack our third item, *salvation*. Salvation happens after we've packed the first two items. During salvation we are delivered from sin and its repercussions. From this deliverance we are given a new way of living. Through salvation, all our punishments for our sins are removed. Once we receive salvation we become new people and should never return to our old selves. In the words of the wise Bishop TD Jakes, "You can't be who you used to be and who you're going to be at the same time."

At this moment, not only does God accept the renewed us, He comes alive within us stronger than ever. We are officially restored. The best part about the item of salvation is that it has no expiration date. It lasts forever, as long as we allow it to work. For this blessing all credit goes to our Lord and Savior Jesus Christ (Acts 4:12). He died once, and for all of our sins, so that we wouldn't receive the deserving punishment of death. Because of His sacrifice, all of our punishments for these sins died with Jesus. And because He died and then rose, when we die, we will do the same. We will rise again, but this time we will rise in paradise.

The fourth essential item for us to pack is our *Baptism*. This baptism is a public declaration of our newness in life. In life we are born into dirty sin. Therefore, this baptism symbolically displays the cleansing of our dirty sins. It's also a public display of our acceptance of Christ and the welcoming of God's Will into our lives.

The final essential item for us to pack is *The Full Surrendering to God*. By doing this you are acknowledging that this life is not your own. Your life, in fact belongs to The Lord. This also demonstrates that without God we are nothing and/or no one. This is the absolute truth! God's Will is the only way of life. Without Him and His will we can't accomplish anything. We must, therefore, try our best to remain connected to The Lord at all times. Once we stop living by our own understanding and let God be the basis for our lives, we can live life more peacefully and abundantly.

Now that we have our essentials packed, let's watch our lives become greatly impacted. Once we have packed with our essentials, we will be allowed to enter the Kingdom of God. Seeing how we are going to the greatest paradise at a discounted rate, let's show our appreciation. We want to be unequivocally accepted into this paradise. We don't want to just squeak by and barely be accepted past the gate. Let's make it absolutely undeniable that we deserve to be there. Let's be honest: we don't deserve this great trip and could never pay Jesus back for it. He has done all of the hard work. We have the easy job! All we have to do is pack the bag to His liking so that we may enter paradise.

That if you confess with your mouth The Lord Jesus and believe in your heart that God has raised Him from the dead, you will be saved. -Romans 10:9

Nor is there salvation in any other, for there is no other name under Heaven given among men by which we must be saved. -Acts 4:12

And he brought them out and said, "Sirs, what must I do to be saved?" So they said, "Believe on The Lord Jesus Christ and you will be saved, you and your household." -Acts 16:30-31

Therefore, if anyone is in Christ, he is a new creation; old things have passed away; behold all things have become new. -2 Corinthians 5:17

So Christ was offered once to bear the sins of many. To those who eagerly wait for Him He will appear a second time, apart from sin, for salvation. -Hebrews 9:28

I am the vine, you are the branches. He who abides in Me and I in him, bears much fruit; for without Me you can do nothing. -John15:5

So we've packed our five essentials items: confession, repentance, salvation, baptism, and surrender. These five items are enough to get us into paradise, yes, but we should pack a few more items that will also be useful. For example, we should pack a mirror. We should continually look into this mirror. By doing so, we will see and remember who we are and what we represent in the Kingdom of the almighty God. In the mirror, we should always observe how we are drenched in the blood of Jesus. The blood covering us should remind us of the power that God has given us. We have been given power to cast away any demon that attempts to attack us (Luke 10:19). With this power also comes a great deal of responsibility. Because we are marked with the blood of Jesus, we are easily spotted by the enemy who wants us dead. We are also spotted by the rest of the society of followers. As followers, we must live in ways that are acceptable to our Lord. We can't afford to fall victim to the enemy's deception and thereby disgrace the Kingdom of God. Since we are covered in the blood of Jesus, we immediately become targets. As targets on this journey, we must defend ourselves, which leads to the next of the packed items.

The next item we should pack is the full armor of God. This armor includes our sword of spirit, our helmet of salvation, our girded waist of truth, our breast plate of righteousness, our shod feet of preparation, and the gospel of peace. With the armor of God we will be able to resist the enemy (Ephesian 6:10-17).

A final item that I suggest we pack is an ear piece. With this ear piece we are able to clearly listen to and hear God. We can listen to His instructions and guidance for us. There comes a time in life when we may be in a place where God doesn't want us to be. It's also possible that we are at a place in life where he wants us to remain. Regardless of the scenario, sometimes we are surrounded by too much noise in life. These noises in our lives obstruct our ability to accurately listen to God. So it's very possible that God is speaking to us and we aren't being obedient because we aren't listening. Honestly, it's like we hear His voice, but we just aren't listening. Yes, there is a difference. As humans, it's very possible for us to hear sound at a particular time, but not actually be listening and comprehending what we hear. It is because there are so many distractions in life. A lot of the noise we are subject to causes God's voice to appear distorted. Sometimes you have to step away from the distractions in your life so you can clearly hear God's voice. And what exactly are these distractions or noises that I am talking about? I'm referring to any action or thought that you habitually take part in that takes time away from God. These noises might be addictions (drugs, alcohol, gambling, sex, etc.), stress, holding grudges, over working, lack of sleep and so forth. If you take part in addictions or overwork, honestly ask yourself, how much of your time are you giving to God in comparison? If you are a person holding a grudge, again ask yourself honestly, what if God held a grudge every time you sinned? If you are a person who doesn't give your body much rest, ask yourself, how much energy do you have to praise and worship God the next day? How efficient are you at fulfilling the task that God assigns you when you're weary? Whatever your personal noise is, step away from it and put your ear piece on. By doing that, you can hear God's voice and follow the path that He has set for you. Being able to hear His voice is solely beneficial for us. Sometimes when we aren't being led by God it can be detrimental to us and lead to our demise. You have to wonder – if we aren't listening to God's voice, then whose voice are we listening to?

The Path

Now that we are all packed, let's start our journey. Let's walk the less traveled and narrow path to paradise. In life, everyone begins at the same starting point. But there comes a time in life and on the path where there is a fork in the road. The same path on which we once easily traveled begins to split. Down one path is where the great majority of people travel. These people could very well be the people who are closest to you. They can be anyone from parents, friends, significant others, children, colleagues, public leaders, and authority figures. What drives them to remain on this most often taken path is pride, greed, and lust. The name of this path is called the world. Meanwhile there is another path which leads to the opposite direction. This one is narrower than the other and not as many people travel it. Where the other path is driven by pride, greed, and lust, this path is driven by faith, love, and righteousness. This path is known as the Kingdom. Statistics show that only thirty percent of the world's people will follow the path of the Kingdom. So what causes the division among groups of people who all started at the same place? In essence, I believe that everyone, in their own way, is looking for paradise. A place of happiness, enjoyment, and bliss. There is just a disagreement on how to reach this paradise. So what causes more people to take the path of the world over the path of the Kingdom? There are a few reasons. For example, the path of the world is essentially the easy way and takes less effort. By this I mean when you can achieve something in the world's path, there's usually an immediate reward that comes from your action. For instance, with drug or alcohol use you experience immediate intoxication or high. With greed you can physically receive or retain your possession instantly. The same is true of lust, which can lead to perversion. From lust you can instantly receive sexual pleasure or arousal. Then there's pride, which can lead to things like anger. Through anger you can physically or verbally react to a situation causing immediate pain. You can see the results instantly.

On the Kingdom path, we rely solely on faith. We may not see our reward instantly or even when we want it. Yet we have faith that the reward will come. The people on the other path operate under a different premise than we do. Their attitude is, "Show me and I will believe you." In contrast, people of the Kingdom think, "I believe that you will show me."

Those of us on the path of the Kingdom have faith that God will deliver on His Promises. Everyone who decides to take the path of the Kingdom should know that it's not an easy route. The surface of our path is far from smooth or flat and is not easy going. While traveling on this path, we will encounter many hills, valleys, and rocky surfaces. If we are able to endure this challenging path, the reward that awaits us far exceeds our wildest imaginations. Our faith is the only thing that equips us properly to make it along this path. Through this path we are given perseverance, patience, self-discipline, and humility. Just because we are equipped for the path doesn't mean it will be easy to travel. It gets quite tough to stay on the narrower path. Even though we are on a separate path from the people of the world, we can still view them as they travel along their path. So while we walk down our path with its harsh terrain, we still watch the people on the other side walking with ease. We still see them receive their rewards and celebrate as if it's the greatest thing ever. This can become tough on us because we can see so many people enjoying a temporary joy, while we still await ours. The fact that we have to work harder for our reward sometimes takes a toll on us. As people on the path of the Kingdom we must be disciplined, patient, and keep faith. Always remember this as the world's people receive their rewards from intoxication, lustful activities, senseless violence, and so forth. These people really appear to be happy. These are the times that some people on the Kingdom's path are tempted to switch paths and may even jump ship. If we observe the world's slogan, "Show me and I'll believe you," we can understand why they receive certain satisfaction immediately. On the basis of this mentality the devil is able to manipulate these people. He manipulates them by giving them his counterfeit blessing. They are truly counterfeit blessings because real blessings are only given through the grace and love of God. So the devil manipulates these people by showing them immediate but faulty. That's why the people on the world's path appear so happy. He gives them a false happiness that never lasts – it is truly a counterfeit blessing. The happiness or satisfaction they receive isn't real. It's fake because it's short-lived and normally ends badly. True happiness and satisfaction last forever. For example, look at drugs and alcohol. For a moment you feel great while you are intoxicated or high. The satisfaction you receive from that doesn't last. The next morning you may have a hangover, sickness, depression, etc. Even down the line, your health will suffer. Because people of the world refuse to change their mentality, they are forced to rely on these counterfeit blessings. They expect to be pulled out of depression or stress. Meanwhile, when we people of the Kingdom are depressed or stressed, we pray. We pray and reach for the word of God. And through faith, the Holy Spirit comforts us. The comfort and happiness we receive for our path doesn't wear off the next morning; it has longevity.

The key to staying on the path of the Kingdom is being humble, obedient, patient, and self-disciplined. While the world showcases its rewards, we must remember to stay patient. We must patiently wait on our true blessings and not cave into peer pressure. The rewards that we are waiting for exceed any reward that anyone can imagine. Stand tall for The Lord, and accept his timing. He won't give it to us until we are prepared. God will not give us anything that we are not properly prepared to receive. While we observe the people of the world, we cannot allow them to distract us. We have to focus on our own task. The task that we take part in will help us prepare for our arrival in paradise. While watching the people of the world, be sure not to join in. We are not of them. We must block them out by using our ear piece. So place your ear piece in and listen to the voice of our Heavenly Father and to His instructions. Notice how He instructs us to be fruitful and multiply. Some people interpret this quote as God referring only to reproducing. This could very well be true; however, I also see it as expanding the Kingdom of God. Display your righteousness everywhere you go and live your life the way God wants you to. We must try to be a blessing everywhere we go. Let's be great representatives of our path, and be walking blessings at all times. Let's also share the word of God with others and try to keep others on the same path. In addition to this, we should try to get people on the world's path to convert.

When we are on this path it's important to know that attacks will occur. These attacks can be quite excessive at both the beginning and end of our journey. Be mindful that there will be a lot of attacks while we travel this path. The enemy does not want us to reach our destination, and will do everything in his power to get us off track. He will try to show you how great the world's path is. He will use people from the worldly path to convince you that you're missing out on something. He will also disguise his representatives from the worldly as people of the Kingdom's path. This is the ultimate deception; contrary to belief, the devil is in church every week. Sad to say sometimes he's even preaching to you. That is why it is vital for people of the Kingdom's path to carry their ear piece and know the word of God. Every person who speaks of God doesn't necessarily represent Him or like Him. Knowledge of the word of God and a personal relationship is the only thing that can save you from this deception.

Finally, one thing that's vital to remember on the path of God is to remain humble. Through this humbleness we are given a clear heart. That clear heart allows us to do things like forgive others who have done us wrong. It is important for us not to hold any grudges. We should forgive people, just as God forgave us for our sins. When we forgive people it's not only for them, it's also for ourselves. It allows our hearts to be pure. It's impossible for us to display the full love of God that's in our hearts if parts of our hearts are being occupied by resentment. So release the resentment, and you will have more room for all of the love that God has intended for you. We should show this love to everyone on both paths. Sometimes that is easier said than done. In truth, there are people who make it hard to love them. We have enemies who absolutely hate our guts and disrespect us. As representatives of the Kingdom's path we are supposed to love them as well. That love can definitely be a challenge. Obviously it's easier for us to love people who display that love to us. Always remember how I said the path wouldn't be a smooth, flat surface. Loving our enemies is exactly what that rocky surface represents. As soon as we learn to receive, process, and act on this gesture, the sooner we'll reap the benefits of the Kingdom (Hebrews 12:11). Most important, as children of God we should love God with all of our heart.

> *But reject profane and old wives' fables, and exercise yourself toward godliness. -Timothy 4:7*

Therefore humble yourselves under the mighty hand of God, that He may exalt you in due time. -1 Peter 5:6

Now no chastening seems to be joyful for the present, but painful; nevertheless, afterward it yields the peaceful fruit of righteousness to those who have been trained by it. -Hebrews 12:11

6

LIFE'S COLORING BOOK

There are times the world can appear to be a very black and white place. By that I mean some people are very closed-minded in how they think and approach things. They feel as though the only way to accomplish things is from the confines of their comfort zone. If it's not in their comfort zone, then it must follow some previous precedent set. The world we live in can be quite complex. Some of us spend our entire lives trying to make sense of its complexity.

The lives we live are like a coloring book that God gave us as a class assignment. It's as if we are in class and He is our almighty art teacher. In this coloring book there is one big picture where the outlines are pre-drawn and determined. This ultimately shows that God has already made us an image of his liking.

So God created man in His own image, in the image of God He created him; male and female He created them. -Genesis 1:27

In this particular picture there is an outline of a tree. After announcing the assignment, the teacher hands the student the outlined picture to color in. The teacher then passes the student a second image of this same outline, but this one has been colored in. The image that the teacher colored uses vivid and vibrant colors. It is absolutely beautiful and looks identical to the tree that's outside the window. The teacher announces that the assignment is to color in the tree outline so that it's identical to the teacher's image. The first image with only the outline symbolizes us before we reach our full potential. The second more vibrant and colorful image is the image God wants us to emulate and strive to become. This second image is symbolic for the anointing he has for us in life. At times, as humans we can be overly confident. We may believe that coloring the image to match God's is an easy task. Some of us are under the assumption that since it's in God's Will for us to reach this ideal image, it'll be easily obtained. Some people believe that it's as simple as just picking up the paint brush and magically creating this image. Actually, it is a lot easier said than done for the average person who is given this task. Achieving this anointing seems quite complex, but with the guidance of The

Lord it can be achieved. Some things we are unable to accomplish alone, but with God we are able.

> *For prophecy never came by the will of man, but holy men of God as they were moved by the Holy Spirit. -2 Peter 1:21*

> *I can do all things through Christ who strengthens me. -Philippians 1:13*

To the average person (non-believer), recreating a real life image like "the tree" seems impossible. When you first start coloring, you have an idea of how it should be. Then reality sets in and it becomes very challenging. The student begins his assignment by picking up the green paint for the leaves. Then he picks up the brown for the trunk and stems. When comparing the teacher's painting to the student's, the two images are not the same. Why is that? Did the teacher have access to a different paint set? Does the teacher not want the student to outdo Him? Why doesn't the student's initial image match the teacher's? The answer is simple. First we must understand that the teacher's (God's) mind and creativity is different from all students (humans). His thoughts and ideas are truly light years more advanced than any student.

> *For My thoughts are not your thoughts, nor are your ways My ways says the Lord. For*

> *as the heavens are higher than the Earth, so*
> *are My ways higher than your ways, and My*
> *thought than your thoughts. -Isaiah 55:8-9"*

There is no comparison. No, He did not have a different set of colors. The teacher will never give His students a task that He thinks they cannot handle. He will also never give His students more than they can bear. What's great about the teacher (God) in class (life) is that He gives the students (humans) the necessary colors and tools to fulfill the assignment (anointing). He provides everything that the student will need to be successful.

> *As His divine power has given to us all things*
> *that pertain to life and godliness, through the*
> *knowledge of Him who called us by glory and*
> *virtue. -2 Peter 1:3*

As students in His class, it's imperative to discover how to use the colors provided. We must figure how to best use these colors to create the image that the teacher has intended for us. The reason He shows us the second image is because He wants us to actually create that. He wants us to achieve that great image that He already has planned.

So right now the student's painting only includes the colors of green and brown. It looks absolutely nothing like the teacher's example. The student must not worry too much. In many initial attempts as students we may fall short of what the teacher (God) wants from us. It's okay; what is important is that we do not give up on the teacher's plan. Never give up on the teacher's plan because He will never give up on us students. He is extremely patient and will always be there when His students struggle.

> *He will not leave nor forsake you.* -*Deuteronomy* 31:6

So here they are with the two images: one is the teacher's beautiful masterpiece of the tree and the other is the student's image. The assignment is for the student to make his painting match the teachers. The student sits there slightly puzzled wondering how the teacher created this vivid picture. He wonders how it is possible for the teacher to create this masterpiece using the same selection of paints. It just seems impossible. The student raises his hand and asks the teacher a question. "How is it possible that we have the same outline for the tree and the same colors, but our images look completely different?"

The teacher replies, "It's because you view the tree the same way as the average person, and not as me. You must understand that you belong to my classroom (Kingdom). As my student, you must understand, think, and view things differently from the rest of the school (the world). Being in my classroom comes with great responsibility. You don't have the luxury to act like everyone else. You are being held to a higher standard."

My Kingdom is not of this world. -John 18:36

And do not be conformed to this world, but be transformed by the renewing of your mind, that you may prove what is that good and acceptable and perfect will of God. -Romans 12:2

The rest of the school sees the assignment for My students as unobtainable and ridiculous. If you show people outside of the class your assignment, they may laugh. They may think you're crazy for being in this class. You should know that they don't believe in what you believe in. Therefore don't expect them to understand you, nor should you give their opinion any value. Most of the people at this school really dislike Me. So expect that many people will ridicule you for even being in My class.

And you will be hated by all for My name's sake: but he who endures to the end will be saved. -Matthew10:22

And you will be hated by all for My name's sake. -Luke 21:17

If the world hates you, you know that it hated
Me before it hated you. -John 15:18

"So would you like to know why your tree looks different from mine? Would you like to know how to make your image match mine?"

Needless to say the student replies, "Of course!" The teacher begins His lecture by taking the student over to the window. He points to the tree outside. Then he holds up His drawing and they compare both images. They both agree that the teacher's tree is identical to the tree outside. The student grabs his own image and holds it up. While comparing it to the real life tree, the student realizes how amateur his painting looks.

Now the teacher asks the student, "Why do you think your image is so different from the real tree?"

The student's response is, "I don't know. When I look at the tree I see green leaves and a brown stump."

The teacher says, "What other colors do you see?"

"I'm not sure!" the student replies.

"I understand that you, the class, and the rest of the school only see one color for images. Now that you're in my class you can't think that way anymore. It's no longer acceptable. So come sit down," the teacher orders. You were not wrong for starting off with green for the leaves and brown for the bark. Those colors are really in there, but those are just one part of the picture. There's so much more to it," the teacher explains.

"Why did you color the tree brown and green?" the teacher asks the student.

The student replies, "Because that's how I was shown before and it made perfect sense."

The teacher says, "Well you were deceived into believing that. As a matter of fact this is not the proper way of thinking. There are always going to be deceivers and false teachers showing you how to do things the wrong way. If they aren't false teachers they could be some misinformed individuals spreading inaccurate methods."

Beware of false prophets, who come to you in sheep's clothing, but inwardly they are ravenous wolves. -Matthew 7:15

Beware lest anyone cheat you through philosophy and empty deceit, according to the traditions men, according to the basic principles of the world, and not according to Christ. -Colossians 2:8

But there were also false prophets among the people, even as there will be false teachers among you, who will secretly bring in destructive heresies, even denying the Lord who brought them, and bring on themselves swift destruction. -2 Peter 2:1

"The reason they were misinformed is because they refused to take my class. See, you were told by the rest of the school that leaves were only supposed to be green and stumps were only supposed to be brown. Well, I'm here to tell you that the art I have in your coloring book is not meant to be simple or like everyone else's. It should be unique and complex. I never intended for you to only use one color for your images. I gave you variety of colors for a reason. I have equipped you with everything you need to be successful in your assignment. So let's look at the colors I gave you. Red, Orange, Yellow, Green, Blue, Purple, Brown, Black and White. In your coloring book, you may very well need to use all of these colors to complete your masterpiece. Everyone's masterpiece is different; some people's masterpieces call for all colors others may not. But you should always be open-minded. You may be surprised at the results when you use all the tools that God has provided you. Never reject the idea of using a specific color of paint because it may not appear to fit in. With that being said, in colors there are three primary colors: Red, Yellow and Blue. From these three colors you can create any other color you need. So separate your colors starting with Red, Blue, and Yellow. Now what colors are left?"

The student replies, "I'm left with orange, green, purple, brown, black and white."

The teacher tells the student he will have to use most of these colors. Then the teacher picks up the orange, green, purple and brown. He throws them all into the garbage.

"What are you doing? I thought that I would need most of these colors?" the student asks in alarm.

The teacher explains, "The factory (the world) presets the shades of these colors and tells us that this is how it should be. Since those colors were preset it could have altered how your painting appears. I would rather you create your own versions of those colors using the primary colors."

"What about the black and white?" the student wants to know.

"Good question!" the teacher says. "Those will be used to adjust the shades of the other colors. I will instruct you about when to use black and white."

The student asks, "Why did we throw away the brown and green? We're definitely going to need those, right?"

The teacher smirks and responds. "You will definitely need those two colors. However, I wanted you to give up your first impressions of those colors because I have a greater plan for you. I will provide you with an abundance of colors and ten different shades of green and brown. So have faith!"

The student asks, "How is this possible? It makes no sense."

The teacher replies, "Have Faith!"

I have come that they might have life, and that they may have it more abundantly -John 10:10

Because of your unbelief; for assuredly, I say to you, if you have faith as a mustard seed, you will say to this mountain, Move from here to there, and it will move, and nothing will be impossible for you. -Matthew 17:20

The problem with many students in this school is their collective mentality. Their mentality says, "Show me and I will have faith." Instead it should be, "I will have faith that you will show me."

The teacher continues the lecture. "Now that I've explained all this, do you have faith in Me?"

"Of course I do," the student say.

The teacher tells the student, "Let's replace the colors that we threw out. Ok so in front of us we have the colors red, blue, and yellow. Now take the red and mix it with the blue. You get purple. Take the red and mix it with yellow and you get orange."

"That makes sense, but what about the green and brown?" the student interrupts.

The teacher's response is, "Be patient, we will get there when I'm ready to show you." The teacher then takes the blue and mixes it with the yellow. "Here is your green. Now mix your red and blue again." They watch as the paint turns purple. "Now add yellow." The mixture turns brown.

"Now take your green and pour ten separate green circles on an empty plain surface. Make sure the green in the center remains its original color. Now add a slight bit of black to the green circle on the right of the center." They both observe as the green becomes slightly darker than the original. "Now gradually add a bit more black to every green circle as you go farther right. Okay. Now take the white paint and do the same for the green circles on the left side of the original. Notice how the green gradually becomes lighter?"

The student sits up in amazement. There are ten different shades of gray, from light to dark. The teacher then instructs the student to do the same thing with the brown paint. After completing that task, the teacher shows the student a different way of viewing the tree. He shows the student the tree's shadows, highlights, and various nuances. "So in the shadowed areas add darker shades of green and black. If you want to make the shadows stand out a little more, add lighter shades of the colors next to it."

Adding the light shades after the shadows symbolically shows hope. Meaning that at times in life we may be in a dark place mentally, or be around others in a dark place. If you happen to be the one in a dark place, remember one this: after every shadow comes a highlight. Hard times are never meant to stay; they are just a part of transition. The shadow is also symbolic of the dark place that everyone around you is in mentally. These circumstances are often displayed in bad neighborhoods, bad jobs, schools, etc. You know that one place where it seems that everyone around you is bitter, pessimistic, or going through hard times. In these circumstances it is important for you to serve as the highlight for these shadows. This is also referred to as being a light in a dark place. It's important that you not get sucked into these people's mindset. As followers of Christ, we must remember to act as just that. We must lead by example; remain cheerful, optimistic, and provide hope to others. By doing so, we may be able to lead these people to Christ.

> *And do not be conformed to this world: but be transformed by the renewing of your mind, that you may prove what is that good and acceptable, and perfect will of God. –Romans 12:2*

Some people may not know our Savior, or may not want to. But because God lives within us, we may provide them with the first or only impression of Christ they may ever have. From our position in God's Kingdom comes a lot of responsibility; we must display the correct representation of the Kingdom wherever we go. Not to mention that if we happen to be in a shadowed area, we must pray that God's Will be done. Honestly, what we are going through may not be for us, it may be meant for someone else. It may be possible that we are being sacrificed in those dark areas. By us being sacrificed in those dark areas, we could be saving and blessing others from the dark. Sometimes in life we may be go through things that we can't understand. These things put us in such discomfort that sometimes we want to give up hope. During these times, instead of giving up hope, we should pray more. Please understand that God's Will isn't always meant for us to understand immediately. Give it time to play out and have faith that there's a greater plan. The very thing that you're going through now may save someone's life later. Through the grace of God you will conquer whatever battles you're facing.

> *I can do all things through Christ who strengthens me. -Philippians 4:13*

Once you conquer that battle, you now have a testimony and experience. With the testimony you can relate to other people who face a similar battle. Through your experience you can guide them out of their battle. As a person who has gone through something similar, your advice can be accredited. With this experience, we can save people as Jesus saved us.

As the student begins to put his final touches on the painting, he accidentally smears the paint with his forearm. The student is very upset, because he was so close to matching the teacher's perfect image. The student sits confused for a moment, trying to think of a possible solution. At this moment one of the student's classmates walks past the painting and says, "There is no way for you to recover from this. The teacher is definitely going to give you a failing grade now! You might as well throw this painting in the garbage."

> *He was a murderer from the beginning, and does not stand in the truth, because there is no truth in him. When he speaks lie, he speaks from his own resource, for he is a liar and the father of it. -John 8:44*

The student leans back in his seat and contemplates his options. "Hmm, should I throw away something that I worked so hard, as my classmate advised? But then again, I can always ask my teacher to help me fix this mistake." So the student decides to ask the teacher for some help in correcting the paint smear. He tells the teacher, "I really blew it, I worked so hard on everything. Now it's ruined, can't be fixed, and now you're probably going to fail me right?"

The teacher says, "Wrong, don't worry about it. Yes, you made a mistake and accidentally pushed the colors outside of the lines. Don't worry, though, I will never give a failing grade for an error like this. Your painting could never be perfect like mine. I only had one student who made the perfect painting."

"Wow, really? Who was He?" the student asks enthusiastically.

The teacher smiles and replies, "He's actually my son. Understand that you will not live up to my perfect expectation."

> *Who committed no sin, nor was deceit found in His mouth. -1 Peter 2:22*

> *But with the precious blood of Christ, as of a lamb without blemish and without spot. -1 Peter 1:19*

"What I like about you is that you tried, and when you had trouble you came to me. Because you came to me with sincerity, I will show you how to fix the mess that you created."

> *But from there you will seek the Lord your God, and you will find Him if you seek Him with all your heart and with all your soul. -Deuteronomy 4:29*

The teacher comes over, grabs the brush, and blends the error on the painting. After blending the error, the image now presented on the easel looks amazing. It is not exactly like the teacher's, but it is still magnificent. It exceeds anything the student could have done on his own.

<u>Coloring Book Break Down</u>

In this chapter contains a tremendous amount of symbolism and I would like to explain it in more depth. The tree, for example. Why a tree of all things? Well, throughout the Bible a tree serves as a very prominent symbol. Starting off in Genesis after building the Garden of Eden, God created many beautiful trees. In the center of those trees were two sacred trees. One gave life and the other provided wisdom. The Lord held this tree of wisdom in very high regard. He held it so high that He instructed Adam not to eat from it or Adam would die. The result of Adam's subsequent disobedience altered the life of mankind forever.

Then there's a section in the book of Jeremiah where the tree symbolizes God Himself. In Jeremiah 1:11-12 it says:

> *Moreover the word of the Lord came to me, saying, "Jeremiah, what do you see?" And I said, "I see a branch of an almond tree." Then the Lord said to me, "You have seen well for I am ready to perform my word."*

In this scripture, God shows you the power of His presence and promises. God wanted Jeremiah to speak to the nations. Jeremiah didn't have much confidence in himself and thought the task was too complex for him – much like the student who received the painting assignment from the teacher. The Lord told Jeremiah that he would provide him with the words to say to the nations. So the guidance The Lord showed Jeremiah is similar to what the teacher showed the student. In both instances, neither Jeremiah nor the student could have fulfilled his task alone. Another correlation is that a preset vision was provided. In the painting analogy, the student received a preset image from his teacher. In the book of a Jeremiah, God provided him with visions. His vision included an almond tree that ripened early. In this specific vision, God is symbolized through the tree. This tree ripening early shows how God will not hesitate to deliver His promise in a timely manner. He will provide you with what you need when you need it. It's said that almond trees tend to bloom faster than most trees. In fact, some can be seen blooming as early as January. They are also said to be able to maintain their leaves for a longer period of time. These facts alone show the beauty of the almond tree and why it symbolizes God. These facts it tie in perfectly with The Lord's statement in the Book of Revelations.

> *I am the Alpha and the Omega, the beginning and the end, the First and the Last.*
> *-Revelations 22:13*

After observing the tree itself, the next bit of symbolism comes from the coloring of the tree. I wanted to emphasize a few major artistic facts with respect to colors. Let's start with the three primary colors: blue, yellow and red. From these colors you can create any color except black or white. Now, you're probably wondering where I am going with this. My point is that every main color (orange, green, purple, and brown) cannot exist without the use of the primary colors. These colors are dependent upon the primary three. In the story, the three primary colors symbolize the Trilogy. So those three colors symbolize God the Father, God the Son, and God the Holy Spirit. The other main colors symbolize us humans. Without our primary colors (Trilogy) we are insignificant and don't exist. The fact that the teacher makes the student throw away the original set of colors is symbolic as well. The original colors of orange, green, purple, and brown were created and set to the factory's liking. In this story, the factory is symbolized as the world. But the teacher instructs the student to recreate those colors using the primary colors. The preset factory colors represent us when we are born into sin. When we are born here on earth, we are viewed as acceptable by the rest of the world. But we are viewed as unclean to the Kingdom of God. So the re-creating of the colors using the primary colors symbolizes our being born again. Notice how once the colors are recreated using the primaries, the teacher shows the student how to recreate those colors in ten different shades. It shows how once we accept Jesus Christ, the things that we vitally need will be given to us in abundance. Another symbolic part of the tree is shown in the coloring of the trunk. Notice how the base of tree is to be colored with various shades of brown. Then notice how the teacher instructs the student to create that brown. He has him mix all three primary colors, red, blue, and yellow in that order. This shows that the base of the tree would not be correct without the primary colors, just as the base of our lives wouldn't be correct without The Father, Son, and Holy Spirit.

The final symbolism that I want to elaborate on is the shadows and highlights. These are displayed through the colors black and white. When you add these colors to any other color, either a lighter or darker shade of those same colors is created. This applies to any color and shows us that we all have good days and bad days. What's important to notice is that the shadows (dark days) wouldn't stand out so well if it weren't for the highlights (lighter days). In life we all experience shadows – some worse than others. I mean no one ever said that our paintings would look exactly the same. However, understand that next to every shadow is a highlight that shows you why the shadow is displayed. With God in our lives, we can get past any shadow. At times the shadow may very well seem unbearable, but God will never give us more than we can bear.

So let's answer the BIG QUESTIONS that so many atheistic and inquiring minds have been asking for many years. "If your God is real, then why does He allow bad things to happen to good people? Why do His people do bad things? Why does He put you through this?" In response to these often asked questions, I'm going to provide you with four answers.

First, let's acknowledge that God loves us all and hates to see any of us hurt. In addition, let's acknowledge that we all fall short of his expectations and that we are sinners. Because we are sinners, we all actually deserve to burn in the fiery pits of hell for eternity. Let's also acknowledge that our God is forgiving and *still* gives us an opportunity to make things right. Let's acknowledge that any punishment we endure here on earth is a small cost. It is a small cost in comparison to Jesus Christ, whose life was sacrificed to save all of humankind.

Second, understand that God allows free will here on earth. With this free will, our enemy is still able to attack the children of God. Let's not forget that we have an enemy whose goal is to kill us. He seeks people who will allow him to use them. And then he uses them to do his dirty work. Yes, you read that correct; he seeks people who will "allow" him to use them. The devil cannot use anyone if they are willing to resist him. So with this free will that we are provided, we are given a choice. We are given a choice to either accept the ideas planted in our heads by the devil, or to resist them.

Therefore submit to God. Resist the devil and he will flee from you. -James 4:7

Finally, my brethren, be strong in the Lord and in the power of His might. Put on the whole armor of God, that you may be able to stand against the wiles of the devil -Ephesians 6:10-11

Be sober, be vigilant; because your adversary the devil walks about like a roaring lion, seeking whom he may devour. -1 Peter 5:8"

One of the biggest misconceptions is that the devil only works through people outside of God's Kingdom. Actually, he will utilize anyone he can get his dirty hands on. As children of God, understand the power that comes with that. Since God lives within us, we have the power to cast out any demon (Luke 10:19). Some people fail to resist the devil and allow him to manipulate their minds. In these situations you will find people who murder, rob, rape, attack others (physically, mentally, or spiritually), participate in terrorist attacks, drunk or careless driving that kills innocent people. All of these things are real life issues that none of the victims deserve. They occur because the enemy is able to work within certain people. In these circumstances, we must understand that we may not have the power to do anything about the results. However, our

God is powerful enough to do something about these things. Indeed, all of these people who commit these heinous crimes will one day feel the wrath of God for their actions. There comes a day when everyone must come face to face with our Lord and account for their lives. To the victims of these situations: know that God is also powerful enough to make things right for you. The grace and blessings He has in store for you will be miraculous. Not to mention that the place in Heaven He has reserved for you is phenomenal. In that special place in Heaven there is no pain, no sadness, no negativity, only happiness and love for eternity.

Third, there is sometimes a lack of self-discipline within people. Have we ever considered that some bad things that occur might have been brought on by ourselves? Honestly, let's hold ourselves accountable for a few things. For some reason, whenever something goes wrong, we humans want to hold someone else accountable. By our being able to place the blame on someone other than ourselves, we feel we can somehow make sense of things. So what happens when there is no one in close proximity to point the finger at? That's when people like to use the Lord as a scapegoat. This is the point where you hear people say, "I don't know why God is punishing me...Why did God let this happen to me? God must hate me!" Have we ever thought of looking at what role we played in this?

As an example, let's look at clogged arteries that result from eating a poor diet. Let's say a person suffers a heart attack. In a situation like this, you might hear people question the love and power of God. At what moment do we question the role that we played? In what section of scripture, whether audibly or in a vision, did God tell you to order the double cheese burger with extra bacon? I highly doubt he instructed you to do this. Same thing goes for the dare devil who wants to tight rope walk across the largest skyscraper in the city. God forbid that person falls off and has a tragic accident. If an accident occurs, you can't blame God. How about the person who continually gets in trouble with his friends? Then gets arrested and must serve a lengthy sentence. Is this God's fault? Absolutely not, that person should stop surrounding himself with the wrong crowd. These are just some of many examples, but I'm sure you get the point. Both the cheese burger lover and the tight rope walker could have been great people. They could have lived great, honest lives, being a great person doesn't mean you can't be held accountable for your actions. The person who got arrested could have been someone full of potential. But just because someone is filled with potential doesn't mean that God has to rescue him every time.

Some people are very narrow-minded. They look at things from a different perspective and say things like he or she shouldn't have gone through this; he or she was such a great person. All I'm saying is that we need to hold ourselves accountable for what we do with our free will.

The fourth point is probably the most abstract and difficult to grasp. It is that God flat out has a better plan for us. For many people this is a hard concept to accept and non-believers will have a field day debating this. All I have to say is that this life really doesn't belong to us. I can hear the skeptics now: "Well you explained the other things, but how do you explain natural disasters, freak scenarios, car accidents, famine, and death at birth?" Sometimes God may call for us to go through things and go places that we don't understand. It's possible that it's not time for us to understand quite yet. Think of it like a parent's relationship with his or her child. As a kid, your parent tells you to do many things that you don't understand. Then they hit you with famous line, "You will understand when you're older." That was a line that I always hated as an adolescent – but it held true in the end. When I was younger, I didn't understand why I was punished for a bad grade or yelled at for waking up late for school. At the time I thought it made no sense. As children, we just think our parents are mean or lack understanding. Once we grow up, we are able to see why we were yelled at for bad grades. It taught us that in life we cannot afford to slack off. And we learned that our lives would be easier the more effort we put into work. As far as being yelled at for waking up late for school, we learned when we grew up that there are repercussions for not being punctual. You can actually lose your job for being late and not be able to provide for your family. All in all, the point I am making is that

God is our Heavenly Father. We are all God's children. So even though we may not always understand why certain things happen, we need to remember that one day we will grow up to be in Heaven, and one day we will understand.

When we go through these things, we sometimes get caught up the moment. We might scream, "Why me? Why me? What did I do to deserve this? Why am I suffering with this disease? Why did my relationship crumble? Why am I a constant failure? Why was I born with this deficiency? Why do I look like this? Why was I given this family? Why can't I afford the things I want? Why do bad things always happen to me? Why does my child have to go through this? Why doesn't anyone want me? Why am I so lonely?" The list goes on, but there is an answer to your question. The answer to "why you" is because you can handle it. That is because God will never put you through something you can't survive. God may allow you to go through tough times because He knows the amount of strength that He placed within you. So the question shouldn't be, "Why me?" It should be "Do I know how strong I really am?" The fact that you're still alive to ask the question "why me," shows your strength. Think about it. If God didn't make you strong enough, whatever you're going through would have already killed you. As children of God, once we are able to grasp that concept, we can then see why we went through it. We are able to see what purpose our discomfort served.

7

A PROJECT FOR THE BOYS

There was once a father who had two sons, one named Anthony and the other, Kyle. Both boys were equally loved by their father and loved each other immensely. They always enjoyed playing together, having fun, and were quite competitive with one another. They also loved to solve puzzles and complete challenges. One day their father presented them with a challenge. He went to His sons and asked them if they would be interested in completing a challenge for Him. If the challenge were completed properly then He promised that they would receive a briefcase filled with precious jewels. Needless to say both sons accepted the challenge. So the father walked His sons over to the site of the challenge. When they arrived at the site, they noticed there were two briefcases hanging from a tree. Each briefcase dangled from a noose strung from two separate trees. Below each briefcase was a pile of six huge bricks. Off to the side of the pile was a bucket of cement paste. The father explained the challenge to His sons. "Ok, boys the challenge that I have for you both is to get the brief-case down from the tree. One briefcase has Anthony's name on it and the other has Kyle's. In both briefcases are piles of the most precious jewels; everything from diamonds to rubies, emeralds, sapphires, gold, silver, etc. If you are able to get the briefcase down, you can keep the reward and use it as you see fit."

Kyle asked, "Well, Dad, how are we supposed to get the jewels down? It's entirely too high."

The father replied, "Use the six bricks that are in the pile below. If at any point you need your old man to give you some advice or suggestions, feel free to ask me. I will gladly walk you through it."

"Great! I can't wait to get started," Anthony eagerly responded.

"I won't need any help; I'm a real man. Real men do these kinds of things on their own," Kyle added.

Their father interrupted. "Well, well, real man, I am going to give you both one full week to complete this challenge. Realistically you both should be done on the sixth day and use the seventh day for resting. That is if the challenge is completed correctly. Don't rush to finish it, take your time. I am also going to give you both this instruction manual on how to as-semble these bricks." Both boys agreed and said that it wouldn't be a problem. "Well we are all set; your challenge starts now!" the father shouted.

Immediately Anthony called his father over, "Hey, Dad, how do I get started and make it to the top? Kyle rolled his eyes at his brother in disgust.

The father said, "You have six bricks. Each day I want you to focus on a new brick. Since there are six bricks I want you to securely align three bricks at the bottom for a sturdy foundation. Then add two more bricks on top of those. Finish up by placing the final brick right on top. By the seventh day all of the cemented paste will have dried and the bricks will be firm enough for you to stand on. At that point you will be able to easily reach your briefcase. Ultimately this will leave the seventh day for resting and spending quality time with me. If you ever get confused, feel free to refer to the instruction manual."

Anthony then replied, "Ok, great, I can't wait. I'll do just that." The father walked over to Kyle, who had already started aligning all of his bricks. "Slow down, son, it's not a race; you're aligning your bricks all wrong. You can't build a structure with only one brick at the bottom. It's not sufficient enough for you to balance. Look at the instruction manual – there are three bricks at the bottom. Then there's two in the middle, and one on top of them all. You have one on the bottom, two in the middle and three on top. This will never hold you."

Kyle interrupted his dad, "Don't worry, I can handle this. You have your way of doing things and I have mine. My way won't take me six days to reach the jewels, I'll be done today."

"If you say so! I'll just let you learn from your mistakes. If you need My help just call out to Me," the father replied.

Kyle proceeded to line up his bricks and didn't even bother to add the cement paste. Meanwhile Anthony was taking his time reading the instruction manual. He took his father's advice and focused on one brick at a time. At the end of day one the father said, "Ok, boys that's it for today. It's time to head home. We'll start back up bright and early tomorrow. Let's see where you guys are in your work. Let's look at Anthony's first."

All three of them walked over to Anthony's tree. He had only one brick laid out with cemented paste. Anthony said, "Tomorrow I'll paste the second brick." Kyle looked at the pathetic lonely brick and began to laugh hysterically.

In a taunting voice, Kyle said, "Are you serious? Is that all you have done?" He was still laughing when he said, "And you actually had help from Dad."

"Well how far along are you?" Anthony replied.

In an excited voice, Kyle responded, "I'm done!" He gave them both a big grin. "Now watch me climb my bricks and go get my jewels." He put his foot on his pile of bricks and started to climb. He had barely put his weight on the pile when the whole thing collapsed and he fell, scraping his knees. Anthony and his father both ran over to help Kyle back to his feet. The father then gave him some ointment and placed a band aid over the scrape.

Days 2 and 3

Over the next couple of days, Anthony kept working on his bricks at a slow pace. He loaded them up one by one. Meanwhile Kyle continued aligning his bricks the same way as before. As the day progressed, he would alter a few things. He tried making adjustments to his previous failed attempt. He tried applying some concrete paint to his structure, but he still failed. Time and time again the father and Anthony would watch Kyle climb the structure and it would collapse. The father even tried giving him advice. He patiently explained how it would make sense to apply concrete paste to a set of bricks that were properly aligned. Each time Kyle would reject his father's advice. At the end of each day Kyle would climb on top of his bricks. And each time, the pile would collapse and he would get hurt. Every time he got hurt, his dad and Anthony would lift him up.

Day 4

Anthony continued to make slow progress on his brick structure. On this fourth day, he examined the base of his structure, noticed that it was sturdy and began to anticipate the jewels his father had promised.

Meanwhile on the other side, Kyle was standing under his briefcase looking up at it longingly. Surrounding his feet was a pile of bricks, which had by now collapsed many, many times. The cuts, scrapes, and band aids that covered Kyle's arms and legs told the story of his failures. After a tremendous amount of struggle, Kyle began to feel as if this mission would be impossible. He became highly discouraged. He glanced over and noticed Anthony enthusiastically working on his bricks.

Kyle asked Anthony, "Why are you so joyful? This challenge is ridiculous and impossible."

"What do you mean, why am I joyful? The question is why aren't you joyful? Our father has promised us these jewels and given us a guaranteed way to receive them," Anthony replied.

Kyle interrupted and said, "I don't know, man, I'm really losing faith in this whole thing. I think I might just throw in the towel."

"Why would you quit? Dad hasn't given up on us; he said that we were both good enough to reach the jewels. We just have to work for it. You have to swallow your pride. He has a guaranteed way of getting the jewels. All you have to do is ask Dad for help and refer to the instruction manual. With those instructions, we can both climb up the bricks, pull down the briefcases, and enjoy our jewels," Anthony said.

Kyle said, "That's easy for you to say; he's been helping you the entire time and you have a perfect structure developing."

Anthony said, "That's true, except it hasn't been easy for me at all. I had to work hard day in and day out to get my structure just right. Not to mention that I still have a lot of work to do. But since I'm always listening to Dad and following the manual, everything is progressing nicely. From the outside you view my structure as perfect. But I'm really struggling to put this together. You're not the only one who has scrapes and cuts. The only reason I'm getting through this is because of our Father, He makes it possible. He never steers us wrong and He always fulfills His promises to us. So if He says the briefcase is filled with jewels and gives me directions on how to correctly assemble the bricks, I believe Him and His words. Just give Him a chance. What do you have to lose? Absolutely nothing, you only have something to gain. Hypothetically speaking, if we follow Dad's instructions and reach our briefcases, we'll get the jewels. And even if we follow His instructions and the briefcases turn out to be empty, we still have accomplished something great and have worked toward greatness."

"Ok, I'll give it a shot! But honestly I don't think I can do it. "

Concerned, Anthony asked, "But why not?"

"There's not enough time. I have already wasted four days, and I don't think that Dad would want to help me after I turned him down. I really don't deserve the jewels," Kyle said.

Anthony said, "Well you're right, you don't deserve the jewels! And neither do I. But our father wants us to have them and wants us to be happy. You just have to understand who our Father really is. He loves us more than anything, and he is definitely forgiving. Remember that time I flushed his watch down the toilet? I mean, He was disappointed in me, but He gave me a hug, and then He forgave me. Then He never brought it up again. He is also very patient. He has been waiting for you these past four days, eagerly waiting to help you out. All you have to do is talk to Him and He will gladly help you out."

"Alright, I'll do it," Kyle said.

Kyle went to his Father and expressed to Him how he couldn't make the structure without Him. The Father hugged Kyle and began walking him through the steps. They began rebuilding Kyle's structure one brick at a time. At the end of the day Kyle had one brick in place and concrete paste smoothly placed on the sides. Anthony congratulated him on his progress.

Kyle smirked and said, "Yeah right. Are you joking? I'm where you were on Day 1. Now you're only a few more steps from being done."

The Father intervened. "You can't worry about Anthony's structure. Everyone will not reach the jewels the same way or in the same amount of time. Everyone is different. Everyone will face their own obstacles. All that matters is that you came to me for guidance, and that you reach the jewels that I promised you."

Kyle wanted to know how it would be possible for him to complete the full structure with only two days left, when it was taking Anthony the full six days. The Father explained to Kyle that he would have to exercise a great deal of faith. "You came to me; now have faith that I will help you complete this structure in the next couple of days."

Day 5

The boys were hard at work on their structures when their Father approached them. He asked them how everything was going. Anthony told him how everything was going great and that he was almost done. He said he just had one more brick to place and that he would be finished by tomorrow. Anthony said that by tomorrow he would be prepared to climb the structure and grab the briefcase. Kyle interjected, "Dad, I'm still working on the base of my structure and I only have two bricks set. But I have faith that you will help me finish this structure by tomorrow. I have no clue how this will happen. I mean completing four days of work in one day is unheard of. But if you say it can be done, Dad, then I believe it will be done."

"That's right, bro. We can do anything with Dad in our corner," Anthony said.

The father looked at his sons and said, "Absolutely, guys, you can achieve anything with me. Now let's go home, boys."

<u>Day 6</u>

The father and the boys returned on the sixth day. They looked at Anthony's bricks. His bricks were perfectly aligned. They were also firm and ready to climb. Then something magnificent occurred. The family turned to look at Kyle's structure and noticed that his bricks were complete. In fact they looked identical to Anthony's bricks. They were just as solid and ready to climb. The boys stood staring in amazement. Kyle was extremely shocked and asked his Father, "How is this possible? I only completed two bricks yesterday. I still had a lot of work to complete. How did this happen?"

The Father responded, "After you boys went to sleep I came back and assembled it. Since you were willing to humble yourself and show faith, I decided to help you. I promised you both that it would be possible to complete the mission in six days and receive the jewels. So now have fun, climb your bricks, and go grab your briefcases."

The brothers climbed their bricks and were able to pull down their briefcases. When they had their briefcases on the ground, they opened them. As promised they were filled with ten precious jewels. Each son gave his Father the best jewel in their briefcase to keep for himself. Then they walked the streets of their neighborhood. The boys passed out some jewels to people who were less fortunate.

Day 7

On the final day of the week, the two sons were done with their task. On this day the family rested, relaxed, and enjoyed each other's company. At the dinner table that night, they shared great stories about their father. They then expressed their love for him and what amazing things He'd done in their lives.

Breakdown of "A Project For The Boys"

Throughout part one of the chapter, there are a great deal of symbolism that I would love to discuss. First there are the jewels themselves. The jewels symbolize the blessings and anointing that God has in store for us. God has many great things in store for our lives. These great things are all in this spiritual briefcase with our names on it. Much like the two sons, we are initially incapable of seeing the spiritual jewels. The only thing we have to go on is the promise from our Heavenly Father. We must have faith that our jewels are really inside that briefcase. Sometimes, because our jewels are hidden from sight, we are unsure of what exactly is inside the briefcase. We are unsure of what blessings or plans God has for us. But by displaying our faith, we are saying that we believe in God's plan and Will for our lives.

Therefore I say to you, whatever things you ask when you pray, believe that you receive them, and you will have them. -Mark 11:24

Now faith is the substance of things hoped for, the evidence of things not seen. For by it the elders obtained a good testimony. By faith we understand that the worlds were framed by the word of God, so that the things which are seen were not made of things which are visible." -Hebrews 11:1-3

The bricks

The bricks are symbolic of a human's life. If the structure of our lives is correctly assembled, then we will be able to receive the blessings that God has in store for us. Some of us are going through tough times. God does not want to see us hurt or sad. He loves us more than words can express. So if we are going through tough times, let's truthfully look into our lives and try to examine the bricks that are in place. We may have to reconstruct our bricks. Can you honestly say that God is at the base of your life? If so, can you honestly say that you have faith in what God has promised? Is there any doubt in your mind that you can receive certain blessings? Then it's possible that you may have to work on your faith. When you have God at the base of your life and truly believe that He will deliver you, then it is impossible for you to fail.

You shall love the Lord your God with all your heart, with all your soul, with all your strength, and with all your mind, and your neighbor as yourself. -Luke 10:27

The Father

The dad symbolizes the Heavenly Father. And just like the father in the chapter, God is loving, patient, and forgiving. He is always there for His children and wants to help by being a part of every decision that's made. He knows what the future holds for His children, and He knows how to get His children there. He will show all of us children if we allow him. He keeps all of His promises and apart from Him we can't do anything. This is shown through the son Kyle who denied the father's help and tried to receive the jewels alone. In life many of us do the same thing. We try to seek happiness through works of the flesh and in doing this we will fail every time. The Father is powerful enough to force us to follow His lead. But He wants us to willingly seek Him. Therefore we have free will. With that, the Father knows that we will make mistakes. He is always capable of fixing our mistakes – if we are willing to surrender to Him. In part one, Kyle did just this. Like Kyle, as children of God, when we screw up we should always remember how our Father loves us. Notice how every time Kyle fell, the father picked him up. He gave him ointment and band aids. God is the most loyal individual there is. Even when we aren't loyal to Him, He still shows us love. What's amazing is that if we surrender to Him with a sincere heart, He will forgive us. We must also remember that with our Father we can accomplish anything. Apart from Him we can't do anything. Just like when Kyle spent a few days creating his structure his own way, it collapsed every time. The reason for this is because he didn't get his instructions from his Father. Once he reached out to his Father he was forgiven and received help. When Kyle put his Father at the base of his life, things started to work out for him. Once we surrender our lives to God there is nothing that we can't accomplish. In part one, because Kyle gave in to his Father, he was able to achieve the impossible. He was able to complete this six day task in just two days. Because Kyle surrendered, his Father not only cleaned up his disasters, but helped him create the perfect structure. Then he was able to receive the jewels (blessings) along with his brother the next day. When you surrender to God, He will deliver you from your trouble. He will then put you in position to receive your blessings.

> *But seek first the kingdom of God and His righteousness, and all these things shall be added to you. -Matthew 6:33*

> *To The Lord our God belong mercy and forgiveness, though we have rebelled against Him. -Daniel 9:9*

For if you forgive men their trespasses, your heavenly Father will also forgive you. But if you do not forgive men their trespasses nei-ther will your Father forgive your trespasses.
–Matthew 6:14-15

<u>Anthony</u>

Anthony symbolizes the ideal child of God. Like him we should be excited for the plans and blessings that God has in store for us. We should also seek God for guidance and refer to our instruction manual (Bible). Then once completed, we must actually apply the in-struction that we've received. With that in place we will reach our blessings like Anthony. The reason Anthony was successful was because his structure was built by the grace of His father. If you notice, he built his bricks one by one. In the first few days he placed three bricks at the bottom. At the end of each day he would apply the cement paste to his bricks. This would allow the base of the structure to become strong. Why is that important?

The strength of the base is important because with-out strength there, the structure will not sustain. The brick at the base symbolizes the trilogy. When we have God at the base of our lives, anything that we develop from there forward will be successful. When Anthony applied the concrete paste to his bricks, he made sure that the relationship he had with the base was solid.

If our relationship with God isn't firm at the base, we won't be able to progress. Then, on top of those three bricks, Anthony applied two more bricks, which symbolize faith and righteousness. Like Anthony, we must have faith in our base (trilogy). We must have faith in our Bibles and the guidance of God. And while exercising our faith, we should also focus on being righteous. Anthony's righteousness not only helped him receive his jewels, but it also helped his brother receive his as well. When his brother lost faith, he worked hard to get him back on track. He led his brother to reach out to their father. As Anthonys in our own world, once we are solid in our faith, we must work on our righteousness. We should be obedient to our Father's instructions, be patient, and accept our Father's timing. Lastly, if we notice one of our fellow brothers or sisters struggling, we should help them and then lead them to our Heavenly Father. Notice how Anthony tried to restore faith in his brother? He could have easily criticized his brother, the same way his brother did him. Instead he provided great insight for his brother. He also showed Kyle that even though he was righteous, he was still not perfect. He reminisced with his brother on a previous mistake and how he overcame it. As Anthonys, even though we are on the right track, we should never neglect or forget our shortcomings. We should not be afraid of previous mistakes, because they made us who we are. By sharing our testimonies, we may be able to save someone else going through something similar.

After the two levels of bricks, Anthony had one more brick to place. With this final brick, Anthony could place his feet and reach for the briefcase. Since God was the base of his life, he was confident that the brick structure would hold him.

> *We speak what We know and testify what We have seen. -John 3:11*

> *Rejoicing in hope, patient in tribulation, continuing steadfastly in prayer. -Romans 12:12*

> *Serve The Lord with gladness; Come before His presence with singing. -Psalm 100:2*

> *Now therefore, if you will indeed obey My voice and keep My covenant, then you shall be a special treasure to Me above all people; for all the earth is Mine. -Exodus 19:5*

Kyle

Kyle represents many of us born again Christians who struggle early before surrendering our life to God. In life we all want to be happy and blessed. There is obviously a right way and a wrong way of going about it. As the Kyles of the world, many of us assemble brick structures that collapse every time we try to reach our briefcases. Have you ever wondered why our structures collapse? Basically the reason is because the base of the structure is incorrect. Anthony's structure had three bricks at the bottom, which symbolized God or the Trinity. Kyle only had one brick at the bottom which symbolized himself. As Kyles we sometimes do the same thing and make ourselves the base of our lives. We believe we can reach the superior plans and happiness through our own understanding. From that single brick, we Kyles assemble two bricks on top of that. When we are the base of our lives, the next bricks symbolize our own desires and personal pleasures. We like to seek the things that we want instead of what our Father wants from us. Through these personal desires we seek immediate pleasure. We can be impatient with God's plan at times. At this phase of impatience some of us begin to think that we can put together a better plan to receive happiness. At this level of bricks, some of us take part in things that we want like gambling, excessive drinking, and sexual pleasures. Once those bricks are in place, we assemble a third layer of bricks. The plan for the third level is that we plant our feet and reach for the briefcase. With the first two levels of bricks representing ourselves, our desires, and our personal pleasures, it's impossible for us to balance the final bricks on top. And even if we do balance them, we will not be able to plant our feet on a sturdy surface. As Kyles we attempt to place the final three bricks any-way. These final bricks that we place are destruction, chaos, and unbalance. The very moment that we go to plant our feet on the brick structure, it will collapse and we will get hurt. When God isn't the base of our lives, we can't receive the blessings that he has in store for us. At that moment we don't deserve his blessings. Like Kyle, many of us reject the instructions and guidance that God gives us. For some reason we think that we can actually outsmart God, or that we know better than God. Truly, as Kyles we must learn to slow down and humble ourselves. It appears that we want God's blessing, but we want it when we want it and how we want. In the story, Kyle wanted his jewels immediately and wanted to do everything his own way. He even mocked his brother for asking for help and working at a slower pace. As Christians we have to be more like Anthony. At first it appears very slow and it looks like the Kyles are doing what they want. It also appears that the Kyles are enjoying themselves much more. Just be patient; it takes time to develop God's structure. But once you complete the structure, you have nothing to worry about. The structure will not collapse or lead to injury. You can confidently plant your feet and receive your blessings. Sad to say, some of us really lack faith in God. Without faith in our structure, we cannot plant our feet and live a balanced life. We must humble ourselves. If we live by Kyle's brick structure, I promise we can expect it to collapse. When it does, we have to blame the base of the structure, which is ourselves. Some people who have the nerve to climb on top of the pile of bricks fall, get hurt, and then blame God.

This makes absolutely no sense. You didn't include God when you created the structure. Why would you include Him when it fails?

> *Trust in the Lord with all your heart, and lean not on your own understanding -Proverbs 3:5*

> *The soul of a lazy man desires, and has nothing. -Proverbs 13:4*

> *The hand of a diligent will rule, But the lazy man will be put to forced labor. –Proverbs 12:24*

Both Sons

In the story both sons reached the jewels, but Kyle had to go a tougher route. In life this can very well be the case. We must understand that God has different missions for each of us. If we endure the struggle then we will reap the blessing that God has in store for us. Sometimes we are really stuck in our ways and make a complete mess of our lives. Just know that God is able to reveal the beauty in every ugly thing that we encounter in life.

Some of us wonder why, as children of God, we suffer or go through bad things. Please understand that God will never put us through something we can't endure. So whatever you've been through, God has given you the strength to remain standing. The fact that we Kyles are able to stand up and even question God's intent, shows you His strength. He could have let you die when your bricks collapsed, but He instilled strength in you. It's possible that if someone else were in your shoes, they wouldn't have survived. However, you did survive because you were strong enough and God didn't let you fade away. He didn't allow you to fade away because He still has great plans in store for you. Understand that as Kyles of this world we are still standing for a reason.

Now let's seek our Heavenly Father and discover exactly what that reason is. From this moment forward, watch your life change for the better.

8

THE SUBMERGENCE

Here I am frantically flapping my arms and trying to keep my head above water. Every gasp of air I take is followed by a galloping gulp of water. So is this the end of my life story? Will anyone even miss me? How did I even get here? I can't believe that I fell for the same trick again. I promised that I would never do this again. Maybe this time I should just let myself drown. I mean, I can't blame anyone if they don't want to save me. I don't deserve to be saved. Can anyone hear me? Does anyone see me? God, I promise if you spare me, this will be the last time!!!

At times our lives can be like taking a midnight stroll on a pier at the beach. At the midnight hour there is darkness and usually no onlookers. We always love to come to the pier and fish. We sometimes do this during the day, but our preference is usually night time. Night time is usually preferred because there is never anyone there to stop us from fishing. So what's wrong with fishing in these dark, cold waters you may ask? The answer is plenty. So much can go wrong on this pier late at night. What if we slip and fall in the water? Some of us can swim, but there are also some who can't swim. This chapter is for those who can't swim.

At this midnight hour there may not be anyone around to save you if you should fall in the water. It's also possible that you could get thrown into the water. Let's be mindful that as humans we do have an enemy. This enemy wants to lure us on to the pier and tempt us to fish late at night. And then our enemy wants us to fall in the water, drown, and die. His goal is to take us away from our loved ones, ourselves, and most important, God.

So what are we fishing for at this hour you may ask? Well, we are fishing for our inner demons – fish that like to surface now and then. We like to seek these fish late at night because it appears there are no life guards on duty. We must be mindful that our almighty life guard is always on duty. Don't think that just because we can't see Him that he doesn't see us. At this moment He is highly disappointed in us.

What do these inner demon fish look like? Well these fish look like excessive anger, money addiction, sexual addiction, drug addiction, and so forth. When fishing for these fish, there is a correlation that we notice occurs, which is how every time we fish, we somehow manage to fall into the water and reach the point of no return. Once we are thrown into the water, the temptations of these fish are hard to resist. And once we are in the water, there are a few possible outcomes. We can drown, be saved by someone, or fight our way back to the shore.

In life, it is vital that we display our self-discipline and not go searching for these fish. Doing so is guaranteed to lead us to a troubled ending. We tend to like to reflect on past fishing trips when we received *temporary* satisfaction. We believe we can capture that same feeling again. Notice that I said *temporary*. The satisfactions that we receive from these fish are short-lived. Not to mention that the value of the satisfaction depreciates after every fishing outing.

> *Now no chastening seems to be joyful for the present, but painful; nevertheless, afterward it yields the peaceable fruit of righteousness to those who have been trained by it. -Hebrews 12:11*

> *Whoever has no rule over his own spirit is like a city broken down, without walls. -Proverbs 25:28*

What is special about these fish is that they ironically hook us after we hook them. Let's observe our types of fish. First, let's look at the largest fish called *Money*. This can be deadly because of its hook. It's highly desired and happens to breed many offspring. These offspring also master the art of hooking their captors. Money is known to breed offspring like gambling, greed, prostitution, stripping, and drug dealing. In life why is this fish so desired? It's because our enemy throws this fish in our face every day. The enemy tries to make life seem impossible without it. When you have this money fish dangling in your face, you start to think you can't live without it. Therefore, many people will do whatever it takes to get it. The desire for this money leads to nothing but evil.

> *And He said to them, "Take heed and beware of covetousness, for one's life does not consist in the abundance of the things he possesses."*
> *-Luke 12:15*

> *But those who desire to be rich fall into temptation and a snare, and into many foolish and harmful lust which drown men in destruction and perdition.*

> *For the love of money is a root of all kinds of evil, for which some have strayed from the faith in their greediness, and pierced themselves through with many sorrows. —1Timothy 6:9-10*

There are moments when the enemy manipulates us into these desires. He manipulates us by showing us that this fish can be quickly obtained. Then he tells us that with more of it, we can reach a luxurious fantasy life. He tries to make it seem as if with this money fish, we will be given a life of paradise that doesn't exist. He manipulates us into thinking that there is a shortcut to receiving this luxurious life. Through propaganda, the enemy tries to show us how Heaven can be here on earth. He tries to show us that flashy things like jewelry, cars, and designer clothes are what should be valued. Don't fall for it!!! Our enemy is extremely tricky and will use the money fish to lure us onto that pier. He will make sure that the deck is extremely slippery. He will make sure to do everything in his power to get us into the water. Then he can fulfill his ultimate mission. This ultimate mission is to kill us and send us to hell with him to suffer for eternity.

The thief does not come except to steal, and to kill, and to destroy... -John 10:10

Submergence Part II

How did my interest in fishing even begin? Let me take you back to a time before I started my late night fishing. In the town I am from we have a lovely beach. It's lined with glittery golden sand and the crystal clear water is filled with an array of fish. On summer days, many people love to come to this beach to fish and have fun. There is only one law about fishing in our town, and that is to avoid fishing the waters after sunset. The reason for this law is that there is a particular kind of nocturnal fish that lurks in the water at night. It is known as the Demon Beast Fish. These fish are known for their sharp horns, sharp teeth, and glittery scales. From a distance they look quite majestic, but when you get up close, they are the most hideous creatures you've ever seen. These fish are highly dangerous and release a toxin called addiction. This toxin entices anyone who gets too close. Once this toxin enters our systems, we are viewed unfit by our Heavenly Father. He is disgusted by the fish and its toxins.

> *The fear of the Lord is to hate evil; Pride and arrogance and the evil way And the perverse mouth I hate. -Proverbs 8:13*

The toxins contain addictions like gambling, drugs, alcohol and perversion. Each fish is controlled by a demonic spirit and assigned to release a specific toxin. When the toxin is released into the air, it gives you an indescribable satisfaction. Once you've come down from this satisfaction high, the fish hooks you with its horns. When that happens, the spirit of the fish takes over your body and uses its hold on you to keep you coming back to the waters at night. Once you begin to habitually visit the pier, the fish plots to drag you under the water and kill you.

As a kid, I often heard this myth, but I never believed it until I became a victim. It all started years ago when I was hanging out with Natas, an upperclassman from my school. Natas had a reputation as a rebel and he was the most popular guy at school. All the girls wanted him. In those days, I would do anything to be seen as the big man on campus. Little did I know that my opportunity would soon arrive.

One day Natas was bragging about fishing at night. Everyone standing around him and listening to his tales was amazed. I heard some girls whispering to each other, "Wow he is so brave! Why isn't my boyfriend that edgy?"

Later that day, I approached Natas and asked him how I could be like him. How could I be popular and get the best clothes, jewelry, and girls?

"Do you really want to know?" he asked.

"Of course. More than anything," I responded.

Natas said, "Hey it's simple, walk down to the pier at night and go fishing. Capture some Demon Beast Fish and sell a few of them. You'll make $1500 per fish. You'll be able to buy expensive designer clothes and jewelry. Save one fish for yourself. Cook it and eat it and you'll be filled with exuberant confidence that everyone will admire. This confidence will draw women to you like mosquitos to light. It will give you all of the riches, women, and status that you could ever want. You'll be the most prestigious man at school."

My mind began to twirl so fast with excitement that I couldn't take it. My gut, though, began to twirl in the opposite direction because it didn't seem right. So I said to Natas, "Hey this all sounds great, but it's illegal to fish on the pier at night. My father forbids me to ever go there at night. If he ever found out that I even thought about fishing at night, he would be highly disappointed in me."

Natas looked at me with a smile on his face and said, "He can't get mad at you if he doesn't find out... Are you a little boy, or are you a man?"

"I am a man!" I screamed, "But I just don't know."

"Well you can just sit there and be a struggling doormat for the rest if your life...or I can help you become the king of this town," Natas insisted.

I gave in. "Fine! Let's do it!"

"Meet me tonight at the pier at 10 p.m. sharp," Natas said.

"What will I tell my father?" I asked.

Natas told me to tell my father that I would be staying at his house for the night. And later that night I did just that.

I arrived at the pier at exactly 10 p.m., as instructed. My stomach was locked in knots that even the most talented Boy Scout couldn't untie. I was going through a roller coaster of emotions. First I thought about all the warnings my father had given me about this pier at night. Then I envisioned myself walking through the hallways of the school with the finest designer clothes and jewelry on. From there I thought about everything that could go wrong: what if I slip in the water and drown? What would my family think? But even as I was pondering that idea, my thoughts were interrupted by vivid fantasy images –images of me being surrounded by many gorgeous women and crowds of people praising me. Moments later, Nata arrived on the pier. We began fishing. It was amazing; the fish literally jumped into our nets as if they wanted to be captured. We caught several fish within a matter of minutes. From this collection we sold all but one of the fish and we made thousands of dollars. Then the final one we cooked and ate.

After I'd eaten the fish, I began to feel this overwhelming happiness and confidence. The very next morning Natas took me to the local department store where I bought a gold medallion with diamonds and the latest designer clothes. Then we headed for school where we, of course, arrived late. The moment we arrived I could feel everyone's eyes glued to us. As we walked down the hall, it seemed as if crowds parted to move out of our way. The feeling I got from this was amazing. Suddenly I was the most desired man at school. Every girl wanted me. This was the very moment that I had always dreamed of. I had everything that I could ever want . . . but there was one problem. I could never tell anyone how I'd obtained my new status. I would hate to be the disgrace of my family. My father would be so ashamed if He ever found out.

With that in mind, I decided I wouldn't be returning to the pier for the entire month. Even though I attended school each day with different jewelry and clothes, I never brought any of it home. I would change back into my usual clothes and remove my jewelry before I saw my family. Living a double life this way was a true burden. By day I was this superstar, and by evening I was just regular Jeffery. The superstar I was at school was amazing, but I began to notice that I was no longer surrounded by my original friends. They began treating me differently. They were disgusted by me and who I'd become. Then at home I was always nervous that my other, daytime life would be discovered. I felt as if I didn't belong anywhere. I'd lost my friends and I couldn't be myself around my family. I never felt so alone in my life. Over the next couple of weeks I got lonelier and lonelier and grew more and more distant from all the people who knew me best.

One night Natas and I were on the pier and I asked him why I felt so bad. I thought my new found glory would bring me ultimate happiness. His response to me was, "Hey all you need is me. All of your friends at school are just jealous. "

I thought about what he said and then I told him, "This night fishing is great and all, but I want my old life back. So tonight is my last night fishing.

"Are you serious!? He replied. "What are you going to do now? If you stop fishing with me at night, I will expose you to the whole city. Your father will find out and disown you. He will never forgive you and your friends will never want to hang out with you again. They will be ashamed to be seen with you."

When he said that, I believed him.

Weeks later I began to realize that Natas was wrong. The more I stayed away from him and the fishing, the better my life became. My friends came back around and I was able to speak to my father with a clear conscience. Life was beginning to go back to normal.

> *You are of your father the devil, and the desires of your father you want to do. He was a murderer from the beginning, and does not stand in the truth, because there is no truth in him. When he speaks a lie, he from his own resources, for he is a liar and the father of it. -John 8:44*

Everything was looking great until one night about 3 a.m. when I received a phone call from Natas. He was breathing heavily and his voice sounded panicky. He said he needed my help down by the pier. He told me he'd snagged a Demon Beast Fish that was the size of a whale. He needed my help lifting it onto the pier. He said if I helped him, he would split the profit with me. He said this fish would be worth millions.

"Imagine all of this money! You can take your family out of debt. You can live the life of your dreams.

Then you can go back into your fishing retirement and no one will ever know," he said.

I told him that I would do it, but this would be my last time. He told me that was perfectly all right. I arrived at the pier around 4 a.m. As soon as my feet touched the pier all of the memories of my previous fishing trips rushed back. I started reminiscing about all of the glory and wealth that I'd acquired when I was fishing. As I approached the end of the pier, my desire to fish became extremely strong. In my gut I felt terrible for being there. I mean I was doing so well. I knew being down there was the wrong thing. And yet, the strength of my desire completely overpowered my willpower.

> *No temptation has overtaken you except such as is common to man; but God is faithful, who will not allow you to be tempted beyond what you are able, but with the temptation will also make the way of escape, that you may be able to bear it. -1 Corinthian 10:13*
>
> *But each one is tempted when he is drawn away by his own desires and enticed -James 1:14*

Just as I reached to pick up my fishing pole, I realized that something wasn't right. There was no sign of Natas and I didn't see any whale-sized fish. I was also thinking about how I didn't want my father to find out what I was doing. And I thought about how I didn't want to lose my friends again. I looked at my watch and noticed it was 4:45 a.m. I decided to throw away my fishing pole for good. This fishing wasn't worth losing everything that mattered to me in life. I flung my pole into the water. At that instant, Natas appeared out of the darkness. He said, "Why did you do that?"

"I'm not fishing anymore," I said. "I want my life back."

Natas's eyes turned bright red and he became irate. He grabbed me and threw me into the water. I struggled to keep my head above the surface and screamed, "Help! I can't swim! Help!"

And just like that, Natas disappeared and I was there alone fighting for my life.

Here I am frantically flapping my arms attempting to keep my head above water. For every gasp of air I take is followed by a galloping gulp of water. So is this the end of my life story? Will anyone even miss me? How did I even get here I can't believe I fell for the old trick again. I promised that I would never do this again. Maybe this time I should just let myself drown. I mean, I can't blame anyone if they don't want to save me. I don't deserve to be saved. Can anyone hear me? Does anyone see me? God, I promise if you spare me, this will be the last time!!!

The night is far spent, the day is at hand.
Therefore let us cast off the works of darkness,
and let us put on the armor of light -Romans
13:12

For there is nothing covered that will not be
revealed, nor hidden that will not be known.
Therefore whatever you have spoken in the
dark will be heard in the light. And what
you have spoken in the ear in inner rooms
will be proclaimed on the house tops. -Luke
12:2-3

I could feel swarms of Demon Beast Fish biting my legs. I struggled and thrashed about in the water for what seemed like eternity. Then the sun started to come up and, miraculously, the entire town ran to the pier to see what all the commotion was. They pulled me out of the water and saved my life.

All week I was all anyone talked about. I was completely humiliated. I wouldn't wish this feeling on my worst enemy. What hurt me the most was that I had disappointed my father. But contrary to what you might think, this whole experience brought us closer together. After I confessed everything to him, he forgave me. My Father even convinced my friends to give me a second chance. I learned my lesson and vowed never night fish again.

After I had regained the trust of my father and my friends I started to realize that Natas was the ultimate liar. He said that my friends and father would never forgive me. He also said that my father would disown me. None of those things were true. My father not only forgave me, he provided me with a life that exceeded my wildest imagination.

> *He who covers his sins will not prosper, But whoever confesses and forsakes them will have mercy. -Proverbs 28:13*

I had learned from my mistake and my father encouraged me to help other people – people who might be facing the same struggles. He told me that the lessons I had learned from my mistakes could be used as my testimony. So I did just that. I began giving seminars where I would encourage people to stay away from midnight fishing. With these seminars I was able to save the lives of people who suffered with this same infatuation.

> *For you were once darkness, but now you are light in The Lord. Walk as children of light (for the fruit of the spirit is in all goodness, righteousness, and truth), finding out what is acceptable to The Lord and have no fellowship with the unfruitful works of darkness, but rather expose them. For it is shameful*

even to speak of those things which are done by them in secret. But all things that are exposed are made manifest by the light, for whatever makes manifest light. -Ephesians 5:8-14

Most assuredly, I say to you, We speak what We know and testify what We have seen... -John 3:11

9

THE BOXER

Yes!!! Yes!!! I made it!!!

The lights are bright, borderline blinding. I swivel my head around and see the boisterous, roaring crowd. They are chanting my name. I raise my hands toward the rafters and my trainer hoists me in the air. He couldn't be more proud of me. Who would have thought that he'd turn a complete runt like me into a champion? Never in my wildest dreams could I have imagined this. Picture this: just last year I was being tossed around and bullied by my enemies. The idea that I will never have to worry about that again is unfathomable. I am not supposed to be here. I am truly unworthy of all of this grace.

So how did this start? About a year ago I was a no body. I was just some snot-nosed hoodlum looking for a purse to snatch and trying to swindle cash. You know, the usual. I was just trying to find a way to survive and search for a little happiness. When I wasn't doing devious acts, I was trying to fend off the neighborhood bully, Big Bradley. It just so happened that Big was a well-known boxing champion in the city. And it also just so happened that he loved to use me for practice. Big always felt he could bully me because I was seen as weak by everyone. Every day he came to me looking to take my possessions. Whenever I didn't have anything for him, he beat me up. Naturally, this caused me not to think too much of myself. I became depressed and angry at the entire world. I was so mad at the world because I felt that everyone in the neighborhood was on his side. Every time that Big Bradley beat me up, people either joined in or turned a blind eye. I felt as if Big Bradley had the entire neighborhood under his spell. No one ever wanted to help me out. I felt like no one ever wanted me around, just because something was different about me.

And then one day something changed.

I was walking up the street and Big Bradley approached. He demanded that I empty my pockets and give him everything I had. On this particular day I was fed up. I was so tired of being scared and I was tired of running. I decided that enough was enough and I stood up to Big Bradley. I threw the first punch. Taking action this way made me feel really good about myself. Well, for a minute anyway. Big Bradley decided to retaliate – and boy did he retaliate. He punched me square in the face and I fell flat on my back. I laid there for a moment gazing at the bright sunny sky. And then this bright sky become dark and gloomy as a thunderstorm of fists rained down on me. Man, these punches were flying from everywhere and everyone. It was as if the entire neighborhood joined the fight. While I was getting pummeled I saw the sky start to lighten up. Out of nowhere, one by one, bodies began falling next to me. Suddenly I was pulled to my feet by a guy who introduced himself as Jesse Christopher. I happily shook his hand and thanked him for saving me. I looked around at the piles of carnage surrounding us. Even Big Bradley lay helpless on the ground, squirming like a fish out of water. Amazed, I asked Jesse Christopher where he had learned his moves. He told me that he learned them from his father, who was the greatest boxing trainer of all time. He gave me his father's brochure and told me to call him. He said his father would train me and teach me to be a great fighter. And, he said, throughout my training, his father would show me how to receive a life full of grace.

I laughed and said, "You're joking right? That's impossible. I am a weak screw-up and couldn't defeat my enemy on his weakest day."

Jesse aid, "No, I'm not kidding. Call my father, he will teach you everything that you need to know. You'll see. He will fill you with the confidence that you lack."

Before Christ enters our lives, we are just like the narrator. Some of us live lives that are unimaginably reckless.

We are also picked on by our spiritual bully, the devil. While he is attacking us, he sends his demons to work through people in our lives. You may notice him attacking you through your family, friends, co-workers, etc. With each attack, our self-esteem drops, depression enters our lives, and stress occurs. But all of that begins to change as soon as we are introduced to our Lord and Savior, Jesus Christ. We come to learn that our enemy doesn't stand a chance against the Lord. There will come a day when our Savior returns and destroys the spiritual bully and all his supporters. Every knee will bow, and every tongue will confess that He is Lord (Romans 4:11).

There also has to come a day when we stop being spiritual victims. We must learn to confront our bully. Accomplishing this can be a nerve wracking undertaking, but it's the only way out. Yes there will be attacks coming from everywhere. And yes, it may also hurt quite a bit. But because you have your savior Jesus on your side, you will be delivered. So right now I would like to encourage everyone to confront their spiritual neighborhood bully. Let's attack our anger issues. Yes, our bully will try to knock us down. He will send people to provoke us and try to make us flip out. But because we have been saved, let's joyfully respond to these negative people. Let's learn not to allow them to force us out of character.

Let's attack our monetary greed. Yes, that bully will try to convince us that our money is the most important thing. The moment we confront him by becoming cheerful givers, generously donating money and tithing, he will want to knock us down. He could very well try to attack our finances. He will try to convince us that donating money and tithing is a bad idea. When that happens, remember that we are saved by God who will replenish our finances. Not only will He save your finances, he will protect the money you gave, and will bless your finances in abundance (Malachi 3:10-11).

Let's attack our perversion. Yes, our spiritual bully will try to knock us down by tempting us. He may send you a woman or man whom you find sexually attractive. He may send you provocative images through social media or television to tempt you. He may send your friends to pressure you into going somewhere or participating in an action that is unbearably hard to resist. Remember, we are saved by God through his word, fasting, and meditation; we will be able to fight off perversion.

Let's attack our drug or alcohol addictions. Yes, our enemy will knock us down and make us feel as though we can't live without our addictions. That bully is the ultimate bully. He will also try to send people to tempt or pressure us into returning to our addictions. But know that any challenge that spiritual bully waves in front of us, we can defeat through our Savior, Jesus Christ. No weapon formed against us shall prosper (Isaiah 54:17).

When many of us were first introduced to God, it seemed impossible we could be delivered. When we are first introduced to God, the devil will send a bunch of punches in our direction. In the same way that Big Bradley beats up on the narrator in this story, the devil has been beating on us so much that it's part of our psyche. As a result, when it comes time to actually train and fight him we begin to doubt ourselves. We believe we are weaker than we really are. We need to erase this stuff from our minds and look at our trainer's brochure (Bible). Let's call that number listed in the brochure. The only way to gain confidence and learn to defeat our bully is through our almighty trainer.

> *"Bring all the tithes into the storehouse, that there may be food in My house, and try Me now in this," Says the Lord of hosts, "If I will not open for you the windows of Heaven and pour out for you such blessing that there will not be room enough to receive it. And I will rebuke the devourer for your sakes, so that he will not destroy the fruit of your ground."*
> *-Malachi 3:10-11*

> *No weapon formed against you shall prosper, and every tongue which rises against you in judgement you shall condemn. -Isaiah 54:17*

Behold, I give you authority to trample on serpents and scorpions, and over all the power of the enemy, and nothing shall by any means hurt you. -Luke 10:19

Training

The week after I met Jesse, I called his father, who agreed to meet me. I was still battered from the beating I received from Big Bradley. I greeted Jesse's father on the street corner and we shook hands. He welcomed me with open arms and told me how proud he was of me for taking this big step. He went on to tell me that one day I would be able to defeat Big Bradley in the ring and become a champion.

I stared at him. I couldn't help thinking he was delusional. "Have you seen Big Bradley?" I said. "I could never beat him!"

The trainer pulled out a mirror and told me to look into it. He asked me, "Son, when you look in this mirror, what do you see?"

"I see a scrawny wimp with a black eye and swollen lip."

"Not me!!!" he said. "Sure, I see someone who has taken his bumps and bruises. But when I look at you I also see a brave warrior who will one day become a champion. This time next year you will fight Big Bradley for the title and will win." (God sees our full potential long before we do). "I promise you this, and I make good on all my promises. My son is the greatest fighter to ever live and I trained Him. He has never lost a fight. I will instill in you some of what he has in Him (The Holy Spirit). By having these principles instilled in you, you will be able to defeat the enemy any time."

We trained all year and we trained hard. There were so many times in training when I didn't believe that I would survive. Yet my trainer encouraged me to keep pushing through. During this process I had to display a great amount of discipline. I had to monitor what I ate at all times and I had to train consistently on a daily basis. The entire time I was training, I felt as if I were giving up everything that I cared about. I gave up greasy foods; I didn't have time to hang out with my friends. I was surrounded only by my trainers and other fighters in the gym. As the months went by, I began to realize that I really hadn't lost anything. By giving up greasy food and exercising I was the healthiest that I'd ever been. By dedicating most of my time to training, I had stayed out of trouble. While my friends were in the streets getting into mischief and being arrested, I was training and getting stronger.

There was one time I decided to take a day off. So I went out with my neighborhood friends. We ate greasy food from this fast food joint. It was an interesting experience. I was surprised to find that I didn't get the same enjoyment that I once got from this outing. The greasy food that I used to love didn't feel right going down. Honestly, it completely grossed me out. At least

I could still enjoy the conversation from my friends right? Wrong! The conversations that I used to love with these guys just weren't the same. The old jokes that used to have me cracking up on the floor were no longer funny to me. And when I mentioned boxing, they looked at me as if I'd grown a second head. I realized that we couldn't really relate to each other anymore.

As born again Christians, we may notice these same patterns. When we first dedicate our lives to Jesus Christ, we notice how uncomfortable it can be to adopt a new way of living. There may be times we feel as though we are losing all of our enjoyment of life. The only reason we feel this way is because we haven't yet expanded our horizons. We notice only all the things leaving our lives, but haven't yet grasped what we are gaining. After faithfully working with God, we will begin to notice a change in ourselves. And this change is truly for the better. We may not notice this change until we try to indulge in our old ways. That is when we begin to realize that the things we once enjoyed don't bring the same satisfaction they once did. That is the moment when we can officially acknowledge that we have been delivered from our past ways. For this great change, may God be the glory at all times. It's like an alarm goes off inside of us when we try bad things. This is the Holy Spirit alerting us.

<u>One Week Before the Fight</u>

We are one week away from the fight. I look at how much my life has changed over the past year. I am so proud of where I am today. I have this new family here at the gym filled with many fighters and my trainer. They all love me so much here at the gym and I love them too. These people challenge me to be a better fighter, hold me accountable for my actions, and help me whenever I am in trouble, where before my friends in the streets had me doing things that could land me in jail. They also allowed me to get beaten up by Big Bradley every day.

I am now in the best shape of my life. My trainer has taught me so much; he has taught me how to reach my full potential and I have all the faith in the world in him. I know that he will deliver on all of his promises. He has taught me that in order to be at my best, I must train multiple times a day. Through these trainings I have developed my strengths and discovered what my weaknesses were. I have learned to turn my weaknesses into strengths. A few months ago I found out that my weakness was my guard. For the next period of training we solely focused on adjusting my guard. By doing this, I was able to defend myself better against my opponents.

For us followers of Christ, God does the same thing with our weaknesses. He will bring our weaknesses to our attention. Then He will work on it with us until it's no longer a weakness. Let's say our weakness is anger. The Lord will keep testing us from time to time on our anger. He may present us with certain situations just to see how we'll react. He will continue to test us on our anger until we pass the test. After we learn to react to these situations without losing our tempers, we pass the test. Through these adjustments we acquire a defensive technique that the devil can't get past. And once we get in the ring, this tactic will mean that we are not as vulnerable. After we've strengthened one weakness, God may work with us on another one. Maybe another weakness is patience. He will work on this weakness until it becomes a strength. He will continually test us and put us in situations that require patience. Such things could be long lines, extreme traffic, waiting on a promotion at work, and so forth. Once we learn to conquer patience, we go onto another weakness. We keep going this way, pinpointing various weaknesses until we are truly righteous and Holy. By then, out weaknesses are either gone, or very hard for our opponent to detect. We will be able to defeat our opponents every time. The only way to reach this point of strength is by constantly working on our craft and our relationship with God. We have to have a relentless work ethic and train daily. You'd better believe our opponent is training nonstop. Our opponent doesn't take any days off. He is constantly working on ways to defeat us. He will take full advantage of any opportunities we give him. He constantly studies us, hoping to find out our weaknesses. He does this so when it's time to fight, he'll be able to exploit our weaknesses and defeat us. So let's out-work our opponent. While he's sleeping, let's work! While he's eating, let's work! While he's working, let's out-work him! We must defeat Satan. The only way to do so is by working with our trainer, God. Study His word and keep praying to Him at all times.

A big part is training is sparring. In sparring we are able to get in the ring and fight a little bit against a temporary opponent. This sparring is meant to prepare us for fighting against our opponent (these are the tests that God gives us). During sparring we discover our strengths and weaknesses. Sparring is also a great indication of how well-conditioned we are and how much endurance we have. It gives us an indication of whether or not we will be able to last the entire twelve rounds of a fight with our opponent. To help build our endurance we, do a lot of spiritual cardio. Things like jumping rope and running miles at a time. It's important for us to build up this endurance because we can't afford to grow weary while we are fighting our opponent. When we get to the 12th round, we have to be able to push past exhaustion and finish off our opponent. In the Kingdom, this is often demonstrated when we go through a spiritual breakthrough. This is the very moment when God is preparing to bless us or progress us. The devil will try his hardest to attack us. He will do everything in his power to defeat you mentally and prevent you from receiving your blessings. In the ring, our opponent might get a sudden burst of energy in the late rounds. We must be prepared to take on any punch that he throws at us. We must also find enough energy to throw some punches back. If we are able to do so, we will be victorious and crowned champion.

During this final week of training, we mostly spent the time watching films and training. During some film sessions, we watched our opponent's footage from previous fights (listening to other people's testimonies). This is the same thing our opponent does to us. He knows our fighting techniques and weaknesses. So we must be knowledgeable of him as well. We must learn to exploit his weaknesses during the fight. Once we are finished watching and studying our opponent's footage, we must become a great student. As a great student we study other great fighters who came before us. So we study the footage of the great Jesse Christopher who was the only perfect fighter in our town. He could dodge punches and respond with powerful hits of his own. By studying his footage I learned and could implement his techniques during sparring sessions. I practiced his techniques repetitively so that they would become habitual and instinctive.

As children of God, we can learn from quite a few greats who came before us. For example, we can learn from people like Moses, David, Abraham, Samson, Jeremiah, Daniel, and many more. We can learn a lot from their experiences. We can learn to implement some of their great attributes in our lives. We can also learn from their errors and try to avoid doing the same thing. In the spiritual realm the greatest fighter to ever grace the spiritual gym was Jesus Christ. He is the one we should try our best to emulate. There is no one greater. Not only did He come to this earth to save us from sin, but also to show us how to live. He has already fought and defeated our spiritual opponent (devil). The devil threw some of his greatest punches at Jesus, and Jesus was still victorious. The devil tried to tempt Jesus, persecute Him, humiliate Him, and even had Him killed. Jesus endured all of these punches and was still victorious. In fact, He threw some great punches at the devil and hit him in his weak areas. Some of Jesus's great hits were His generosity, His love, His forgiveness, His self-discipline, and His service. These were just a few of the punches, there were many more. Jesus delivered these punches all the way up to His death and the devil hated it. His generosity was shown when He gave bread to the masses. His love was displayed everywhere He went. It's truly impossible to list off every example. Through His love, He was able to forgive the people who persecuted Him. This gave Him the ultimate strength. How many people can honestly endure the torture that He did? He faced everything from insults, punches, kicks, being nailed to a cross, and dying. He is the strongest fighter to walk this earth. Not only because He endured that, but because after all the torture, He still showed love. He had enough strength at the end to ask God to forgive His enemies.

One of the greatest knockout punches Jesus delivered to the enemy was His self-discipline. Not only did He resist the devil's temptation, He stuck with God's plan. Even on the last day, the devil tried to get Peter to talk Jesus out of going to the authorities. When he rejected Peter's suggestion, it drove the devil crazy. It really showed Jesus's determination to save the lives of every sinner. The final punch that Jesus delivered to the devil was through His service. Everywhere Jesus went He led by example and performed great miracles. He was literally a walking blessing. Everywhere He went He healed people, fed people, taught people, saved people, cleaned people's feet, or did some other selfless deed. Jesus delivered these punches all 12 rounds until it wore His opponent down. He utilized this punch until the final bell rung. While He was dying on the cross, He saved another man who was also nailed on the cross next to Him. At the end of the fight, Jesus was victorious. He received His championship belt three days later when He rose from the dead.

Fight Night

The night of the fight I was slightly nervous. I mean everything that I had worked so hard for would come down to this one moment. This was the moment that I had been waiting for, for so long. Big Bradley had beaten me up so many times, and now I would have the perfect opportunity for revenge. So I began to think about different possible scenarios. I envisioned myself knocking Big Bradley out in the first round and then watching him beg for mercy. I also imagined Big Bradley knocking me out in the first round as he'd had plenty of experience doing in the past. This didn't exactly help my nerves; however, my trainer assured me that I was prepared and ready to defeat the opponent. Then He reassured me that if I needed anything, He would be in my corner instructing me along the way. With Him I could accomplish anything (Philippians 4:13). He said, "Hey, I prepared you for this moment, the opponent has already been defeated. All you have to do is follow my game plan.

The moment I stepped inside the ring, all the nerves I'd previously had disappeared. My trainer had instilled so much confidence in me. In the first couple of rounds I tried to test Big Bradley out. I sat back and observed what kind of punches he threw. I then began to throw a couple of punches just to see what made him drop his guard. I tried to notice patterns and flaws in his defense technique. By observing my opponent's tendencies, I would be able to plot how I could deliver my power punches.

When I got to the mid rounds, I began to notice that my opponent really knew me well. He began to target four different areas that were once considered my weaknesses. The opponent didn't realize that my trainer had worked on these exact weaknesses with me. So I wasn't as vulnerable in these areas as I once was. For those mid rounds, Big Bradley really went after those weaknesses. The more he targeted these weaknesses, the more frustrated I became. He began hitting me with some very powerful blows. With one of them, he cut me over the eye and I began to bleed. At that moment I began to neglect everything that I had learned in training. My trainer kept shouting from the corner. "Use your counter, use your counter." Foolishly I ignored Him and wildly threw punches that never landed. This is when I saw the fight begin to slip away from me. The blood from the cut was leaking into my eyes. I couldn't clearly see my opponent, who took advantage of that eye. He aimed for my eye for several rounds.

In the spiritual realm, this happens when we haven't yet truly conquered all our weaknesses. We can definitely expect the devil to keep attacking us in these areas until we successfully defend them and throw some counter punches. If we allow him to exploit our weaknesses the way the narrator did, we will definitely have our own version of blood in our eyes. This will cause our vision to be tainted. When our vision is tainted as Christians, the devil is able to place doubt and deception into our lives. Once this occurs, he will try to get us to step away from the game plan that God has for our lives. He will try to get us to abandon what we learned from the Lord in our training. He wants us to think that we can beat him without listening to our trainer in the corner. This is absolutely impossible to do. Only through our trainer can we defeat our opponent (John 15:5).

At the end of the eleventh round I sat in the corner with my trainer who gave me water. He said, "What are you doing? You're blowing the fight, you're not doing anything that we practiced, and you're not listening to my instructions. If you want to win this fight you'd better straighten up. Start throwing counter punches. When he throws the punch of greed, counter with generosity. When the devil tries to tell you to keep all of your money and do whatever it takes to get more, you counter by always tithing your first and best ten percent to God. You also counter it by donating and giving to the less fortunate. When he throws the punches of lustful desires, you counter it with self-discipline. Don't indulge in the ways of the world. When he throws punches of anxiousness, throw the counter of patience. Remember this, because when he throws the anxious punch, he's trying to set up for the knockout punch of pride. When he delivers the knockout punch of pride, counter with your own knockout punch of humbleness...If you do this, kid, you will win the fight...you have to knock him out this round. If you don't knock him out, the fight could come down to a split decision by the judges and their scorecards."

In sports like boxing, when there's a split decision it basically means that the destiny of your fight is dependent upon the judges. When you win by unanimous decision, it's pretty much obvious who has won the fight. The person who wins by unanimous decision has, according to the judges, undeniably defeated his opponent. There's also a decision called the split decision, which isn't as obvious. In the split decision the judges are kind of indecisive; the winner of the fight is not obvious. In this situation the judges can make valid points about why each fighter deserves to win the fight. So they arrive at their judgement for a winner by nitpicking every little point of the fight. The fight comes down to each judge's scorecard for each round. In the spiritual realm, we want to beat our opponent (the devil) to a bloody pulp and leave him unconscious. We don't want him to have a place in our lives. In our spiritual fight with the devil, we can't afford to allow our fight to be a split decision. This split decision could possibly cost us a trip to Heaven. When we approach the gates of Heaven we want God to have an obvious decision/reason to let us into Heaven. We shouldn't put Him in a position to give a split decision on whether to let us in or not. He shouldn't have to weigh all the negative and positive things we did in our lives. He should be able to look at us and see a clear cut winner. So with that in mind, let's not give the devil any room to maneuver in our lives. Let's finish him off. We will therefore be able to enter Heaven with ease instead of barely making it. Let's not risk our spot in Heaven for this coward. Let's demolish our opponent while we are still breathing. In addition, never accept the idea of being "good enough." In life we should always strive to be greater.

As the twelfth round progressed the opponent threw the exact punches that my almighty trainer warned me about. He threw the punches of pride, greed, and lust often. I was able to resist those punches and applied my own counters. I also landed some great punches to his head. I can't lie; by the final minute of the twelfth round was exhausted. It appeared that Big Bradley was throwing punches faster and stronger by the second. He was giving me everything that he had and he wouldn't let up. During this array of punches I began to feel my body wear down. I wanted to give up so badly. The enemy not only threw his signature punches, he threw a few surprise punches as well. He threw a punch at my health, a punch at my finances, and a persecution punch. I thought I might lose the fight. That is, until I heard my trainer shout, "Don't give up!!! Keep pushing!!! Give him everything you have left and I promise you will be victorious and will be crowned champion." (Galatians 6:9) Those were the magic words that I needed to hear. I had complete faith in the words of my trainer, so I threw him everything I had left in me. I started throwing my power punches. Then there were only ten seconds left on the clock and the crowd was roaring. I was in the center of the ring with my body battered with bruises, cuts, and blood. I squared off with my opponent Big Bradley. In the past he had beaten me up so many times. I wasn't going to let that happen again. He was the only thing standing in the way of me and the championship belt. I looked him in the eyes with complete disgust. I then uttered the words, "I rebuke you." Then I threw every punch I had left in me. I threw the punches of forgiveness, love, generosity, faith, and patience. After this barrage of punches, my opponent dropped to the ground and I trampled over him. The bell rang. The crowd stood in amazement, ecstatically cheering for me. My trainer handed me the championship belt and raised my hand into the air. I stood there in the ring as the new champion, just as my trainer had promised. There's no way I could have done this without Him.

In life when we are going through a spiritual breakthrough, it is as if we are going through our own spiritual version of a twelfth round. The devil at this stage will try anything in his power to knock us off track. He will try to hit us in various places in our lives. He will try to get us to doubt God's plan, God's glory, and our love for God. He will try to destroy all of the hard work that God has done in our lives. He will try to physically, mentally, and spiritually kill us, so we will no longer be considered a threat. This is when we must endure everything the devil throws at us. With God we can accomplish this. The devil is not powerful enough to stop God's blessings. He will try to trick us into missing out on those blessings or God's plans. The only reason he attacks us so hard is because he knows the greatness that God has in store for us. He doesn't want

God's tremendous will to be done. He even tried this with Jesus. Before Jesus was crucified, the devil tried to get Peter to talk Jesus out of the plan. This time period was symbolic of Jesus's twelfth round. In this round, Jesus was able to endure those final punches and fulfill God's plan.

> *I can do all things through Christ who strengthens me. -Philippians 4:13*

> *I am the vine, you are the branches. He who abides in Me, and I in him, bears much fruit; for without Me you can do nothing. -John 15:5*

> *And let us not grow weary while doing good, for in due season we shall reap if we do not lose heart. -Galatians 6:9*

10

THE ARMY

As followers of Christ, the very moment that we are saved, we are enlisting in God's Great Army. This army is the most prestigious and yet the most hated. The reason for both is because this army cannot be defeated. We are led by the Almighty General who created the entire Universe, Heaven, and Hell. By joining this army we are instantly marked men and women. The moment we decide to enlist, the enemy immediately attacks more than ever. The enemy will fire shots at you and try to intimidate you. He wants you to believe that you made the wrong decision. Never fall for this; stand tall for the Lord and become a strong soldier. A lot of responsibility and persecution comes with being a soldier in this army. In the end the reward is well worth it. In this army we are responsible for not only ourselves, but also for our brothers and sisters in Christ.

We must understand what an honor it is to be in the army. We are a privileged bunch of people. With this privilege comes much responsibility. As soldiers we must exercise a great deal of self-discipline, patience, perseverance, and integrity. All four of these things can be extremely challenging to exercise. However, it is possible that with the proper amount of effort we can all be great soldiers. While we are in boot camp we learn what it takes to be a great soldier. There is already a layout on how to successfully acquire the traits needed to be a great soldier. Not only are we in the greatest army led by the Almighty General, but He has assigned us the perfect Squad Leader in Jesus. He is the only soldier who was perfect. We could never live up to His perfection. But if we want to be successful soldiers we should follow the example that He has set. He has experienced every obstacle there is in battle and overcome them. From His experiences He shows us the proper techniques to win those battles. We have a perfect role model and our goal is to emulate His examples. In the beginning stages of boot camp our squad leader shares with us the traits we will need to be successful. They are: Obedience, Love, Faith, Patience, Self-discipline and Knowledge. By acquiring these six traits we can defeat our enemies "6s" that are placed on his marked ones. Where our enemies are marked with the 6s, we are marked by the blood of Jesus. By being marked with the blood we should acquire these traits and maintain them. Just as Jesus did.

One of the first traits that we should pay close attention to is knowledge. Not to sound cliché, but in this army, knowledge is absolute power. As soldiers we should be knowledgeable in the word of God. In this way, we can better defend ourselves from the enemy. One of the strongest weapons that our enemy will shoot at us is deception. The enemy will fire shots at us trying to cause confusion and uncertainty. He will first try to deceive us by dressing in disguise and planting wrong ideas in our mind. He will tell you that you're not good enough, you're ugly, you can't be forgiven, and he will try to get you to blame God for his actions. Through the acquisition of proper knowledge you can learn to defeat the enemy. When the enemy says, "You're ugly," God says, "I made you beautiful." When the enemy says, "You're not good enough," God says, "You can accomplish all things through me, because I will give you strength." When the enemy says, "You can be forgiven," God says, "If you repent, I will forgive you." When you're going through tough times, the enemy will try to get you to curse God's name and blame Him. His ultimate goal is to separate us from our army by using our own ignorance against us. So be knowledgeable in what The Lord says. It is truly important because we are getting ready to face a great battle soon. Before Jesus returns, we will have a very treacherous battle against the enemy. During that time period there will be a lot of people in high positions who will try to mislead you. They will give you inaccurate information and try to separate you from our army. There will be preachers telling you incorrect information. Some people think being a good soldier only means going to church every Sunday. I'm going to be honest with you, it takes more than that. Going to church every Sunday will not secure you a place in Heaven. There are people who go to church every Sunday who may burn in Hell. That is because they are not knowledgeable about, or obedient to, the laws of our army. It's also possible that they're more knowledgeable than we think. They could be using their church attendance like guerrilla warfare and as sneak attacks. By this I mean that our enemy attends church every Sunday also. And worse, sometimes the enemy is disguised as our own soldiers and preaches to us. Being a soldier for Christ is something that we must be 24/7. Some people have already been deceived and believe that it's okay to act however they want six days out of the week. Then they think that lacing up the army boots every Sunday classifies them as great soldiers. We must be held accountable for our actions at all the times.

This brings me to the next aspect of being a successful soldier – self-discipline. Self-discipline goes hand in hand with integrity. We must discipline ourselves to act in ways that make our Almighty General proud at all times. We must make a valiant effort not to bring any shame to the army. Honestly the biggest part of being a great soldier is to play the part of a great soldier. We must apply our training every day in life and never let up. The enemy we are fighting is the exact opposite of us. He represents the opposite of everything we stand for. Therefore it's not appropriate for us to take part in practices of the opposition. We can't live like the enemy Monday through Saturday and reap the benefits of our army on Sunday. If we more like our enemy than ourselves, what does that say about us? By not properly representing our army we can scare off or confuse others. The people we could confuse are those people who are thinking about enlisting, our own soldiers, and opposing troops. By not properly representing our army, you give people a reason to question our principles. Furthermore, you can cause our soldiers to jump ship and join the enemy. It's easy to understand why we must display our self-discipline at all times. Don't take part in the actions of our enemy. Don't get intoxicated, commit adultery, steal from others, or harm others or yourself. I know these things can be hard when you're surrounded by temptation. As soldiers of the Kingdom, we must learn to distance ourselves mentally and physically. You have heard it said, and it is completely true: the true measure of a man or woman is not what they do when people are watching, but what they do when they are alone. We must practice self-discipline and we must have the integrity to not take part in ludicrous activity. What's so fantastic about our army is that we have been appointed a squad leader who has succeeded at this. Jesus was faced with temptation and was given the opportunity to behave like the opposition. This occurred when Satan tempted Him in the woods. Jesus resisted and didn't take part in the acts with which He was tempted. Because Jesus has already been through the trenches and emerged victorious, we should listen to His, the Holy Spirit's, and God the Father's instructions.

After self-discipline, practice the next key trait of obedience. As our Almighty General, God never gives us instructions that aren't in our best interest. One of the greatest attributes every soldier must acquire is the ability to listen and obey directions. One simple lapse of judgment with disobedience could result in death – not only for you, but for your fellow troops. We must therefore honor who we are and what we stand for. In basic training we are taught the creed that we shall abide by and follow.

The Creed

I am a Christian Soldier in the Kingdom of God

I shall have no other God before the Almighty God

I shall not make idols

I shall not take the name of The Lord God in vain

I shall remember the Sabbath day to keep it holy

I shall honor my father and mother

I shall not murder
I shall not commit adultery
I shall not steal
I shall not bear false witness against
my neighbor
I shall not covet
I am a Christian soldier in the Kingdom
of God
(Exodus 20:2-17)

If we can abide by this creed, we will be held in high regard in this army. In addition to abiding by this creed, our Almighty General instructs us to obey all authority figures. In life sometimes we can have too much pride and feel entitled to certain things. As men and women of Christ, we must learn to humbly submit to authority. This especially goes for people who consider themselves leaders. How could you possibly expect people to follow your direction when you haven't learned to submit to authority? We must understand that just because we live in this world doesn't mean that we are of this world. We belong to an opposing Kingdom with different principles. Whenever you're unsure about how to react in certain situations, follow your squad leader's example. Let's not forget that the squad leader was perfect and always did everything perfectly. If you pay attention, you'll realize He was extremely obedient to the authorities. The entire time that he was being persecuted, He knew that He was innocent. He knew that He never committed any of the crimes that He was accused of. Our Squad Leader Jesus also had the power to stop the persecution. But instead of stopping it, He humbly submitted to the authorities. He allowed the officers to shackle Him. He accepted the punishment given to Him, which was His crucifixion. Jesus showed great strength because He had the power to avoid death, but He still humbly submitted. We must understand that Jesus was a perfect soldier. He died in honor of our Kingdom. He was always obedient and definitely lived correctly by our creed. To be specific, during His crucifixion He honored the sixth line of our creed (the fifth commandment), "I shall honor my Father." So when He submitted to the authorities, He was also obeying His Father, The Almighty General (God the Father). In order for us to be successful soldiers we must follow the Lord's instruction. Being obedient for some of us can be quite challenging at times. That is because we don't always see immediate results. Please understand that although we may not see results when we want, they will always come in time. As a way to help make Obedience easier we must have faith in our Almighty General. Our General doesn't even require a lot of faith. He said that we only need the amount of faith of a mustard seed (Matthew 17:20). We need to have faith that everything we are going through serves a purpose. We must have faith that God is in the process of answering our prayers.

This leads to the next trait all good soldiers must have: Patience. You can't pray to God to do something in your life and demand that what you've prayed for happens immediately or magically appears in front of you. Don't get me wrong, He can definitely make that occur for you. But sometimes He wants us to go through a process first, one that will prepare us for the blessing that we prayed for. He's not going to give you something that you're not prepared to handle. I promise I wouldn't be saying this if I weren't a living testament to this. For as long as I can remember, God has communicated with me through visions or basic gut instinct (provided by the Holy Spirit). He has always shown me large crowds of people whose lives I would impact. I've had this vision since about the age of five, and it is very vivid. I always had faith that I would obtain this stature. I just didn't know how. I used to tell people that I would impact many lives one day and be a huge figure. I heard things like, "Think realistically... don't quit your day job...use your college degree and get a job with benefits."

From my perspective, I *was* thinking realistically, and the visions that were planted in my head exceeded any doubts these people suggested. There was one point in my life when I had some slight doubt in my vision. The doubt came even though I kept faith. As I grew up not only in age, but spiritually, I gained an understanding of why that doubt had come.

As a kid I always thought these visions came from my own mind. As I got older, I learned that these visions actually came from my Almighty General. I came to this conclusion a few months after I graduated from college. There I was alone in my room staring at the wall feeling like an ultimate failure. My whole life I had envisioned bright lights and a big platform. The enemy began planting doubts in my head. I began to think, *look at me, twenty-two years old, living at home with my mom...I should be famous with great success by now...maybe I should just do what everyone else said I should do – get a job with benefits and forget about these visions.* Yes I know, twenty-two is young, but remember I started having these visions at age five. So after seventeen years I felt discouraged because I had prayed for this success every day of my life. At this point I felt like God didn't hear me. I decided to take matters into my own hands and apply for a job as a business recruiter. This job would give me benefits and set me up with a pension. Within a week I had gone on two interviews for this job. It seemed as if everyone on the hierarchal ladder loved me. During the interview process, I met with everyone from supervisors, managers, and Regional Vice Presidents. I was told that I was a top candidate for the position. So I waited by the phone for a month and never received a call back. Then I prayed to God and expressed to Him how lost and alone I felt. Within moments, He made sense of everything for me.

"Mike, follow my voice; I planted these visions in your head for a reason. Follow my voice. The moment you saw these visions you began to pray to be successful and achieve this vision. Follow my voice. You prayed for these visions to come true and to be successful. Follow my voice. I have been answering your prayers and making you take of the necessary steps to achieve these visions. Follow my voice. I need you to have faith in me. Be patient because this takes time. Follow my voice. You were more than qualified to land the business job, but that wasn't in the vision. So follow my voice, have faith, and be patient."

Hearing this definitely restored a confidence in my faith. I began to pray fervently, meditate, read my Bible, and listen to the teachings of my favorite speakers, Joyce Meyer and Bishop TD Jakes (via the internet). With this restored faith, I began to understand that God really wanted me to obtain this vision; I just needed to be patient. About a month later, I got the urge to go to New York City alone. Here is where my faith would be measured. I admit at this moment I was a bit impatient and impulsive. For some reason I thought that I could make God's vision happen on my own. I was determined to go to NYC and leave with a new job position in the entertainment industry. I made a vow to myself that I would not comeback empty-handed. I bought the cheapest flight and the cheapest hotel I could find in Queens, NY. The hotel I went to was infested with ants and smelled funny. Nevertheless, despite my being annoyed, I was satisfied with it. I had faith that this was the trip where God would show me His greatness. So that week I mapped out a schedule that I thought would land me a step closer to my vision. One day I sat in the audience at a televised music video countdown show. I sat in amazement in the crowd and envisioned myself as the celebrity answering all of the tough questions.

The next couple of days I attended a few acting auditions. I went to all of these auditions and failed to land any roles. During one of them the casting director read a newspaper. She paid absolutely no attention to me. Later that day I went to a late night talk show and sat in the audience. This was the best thing I'd ever witnessed. Again I visualized myself sitting, answering these tough questions and promoting my latest projects with this famous interviewer. Doing that boosted my confidence to the next level. The following day I decided to go to every record label and TV network to pass out my resume. I did this from 8 a.m. to 8 p.m., hoping to land a job. I was kicked out of every building that I attempted to get into. Later that night I went to a pro sports draft and sat in the crowd. I watched many college athletes' dreams and visions come true. Witnessing this left me with an interesting feeling. One part of me couldn't help but wonder when my day would come. Another part of me was ecstatic because I now had visual proof that dreams could come true. On my last day in town I reminded myself how I couldn't go home empty-handed. There I was on my last day in the big apple with absolutely no ideas left. As I walked the streets of Manhattan, it was placed upon my heart an impulse to stop into this random cafe. I grabbed a table on the second level and sat there feeling like an absolute failure. I reflected on the fact that I had spent my last dollar to come to this city, stayed in a filthy hotel, slept an average of four hours a night, awakened at 5 a.m. every morning just to receive rejection after rejection. I began to question God and asked Him what the point of this trip was. Why would I go through all of this just to fail and go home empty-handed?

He told me, "You're not going home empty-handed."

I said, "I tried everything in the book and still failed." I went on to say, "I need you, Lord. I have faith in your vision for me, but I can't do it without you. Just give me a sign about how I will fulfill this vision."

He said, "That was the entire point of this trip. I wanted you to come to the realization that you cannot do it without me. I had to break down your previous mindset so that I could rebuild it from scratch." After receiving this message, I experienced the most vivid dream that I'd ever had. This time it felt as if I were physically living it. In this vision I was the person I'd always imagined and dreamed about being. The only difference was that this time it felt all too real. After these visions occurred, ideas began pouring into my head about how I would reach this level of success.

These ideas were pouring into my head so fast that I couldn't keep up with them. I reached into my pocket and found a tiny piece of scrap paper. I wrote down all of these ideas. I wrote as small as I possibly could so I could fit all of the ideas on the paper. I couldn't keep up with the thoughts. From this experience, there was no doubt in my mind that God was really with me. I then realized that with faith and patience I could accomplish anything. So there I was in the cafe with my vision and instructions on how to obtain it on a tiny scrap of paper. I began to cry tears of joy. This is something that I'd never experienced before. I have never really been a crier. Honestly the last time I probably cried before this moment in the café was after birth. Okay, maybe there were a couple of times in between – but this was truly a rare occurrence. This is when I realized that God had a lesson for me that would break me down. Through this breakdown He would show me His greatness. It also showed me that I couldn't achieve anything without him. This was an astonishing thing to experience. I not only trusted God, but I felt a love for Him like never before.

From this moment I discovered one of the final traits of a great soldier is Love. As soldiers we must love people. We must love God, ourselves, and everyone else – even our enemies. We must love everyone. If there is anyone struggling we should help them out and lift them up. Never look down on someone unless you're reaching down to pull them up. We must love people the way that God loves us. This love opens up our hearts up. With this opening we will be more receptive to doing miraculous things such as forgiving others. A great example of this was shown through God, who loved us so much that He sent Jesus to be sacrificed for all of us troops (John 3:16). Through this sacrifice all of us were forgiven for our sins and saved from the fiery pits of Hell. Jesus was filled with so much love that after being tortured, after having His hands and feet nailed to the cross, he still found the strength to exhibit His love. He showed love and compassion to the people who were harming Him. He asked God the Father (Almighty General) to forgive His enemies. This gesture alone showed the tremendous strength of the greatest soldier.

Look After Your Brother and Sister Soldiers

What gives God's army more strength is the love and care that we share among each other. When you see your brother down, don't join the persecutors; instead lift him up. Don't allow division within your platoon. The division will lead to your destruction. There are times at war when one of us may be wounded. We shall never leave one of our brothers or sisters behind. Even if they have been captured by the enemy, never give up hope. Fight for them and show the resistance that our Squad Leader, Jesus showed us. There are moments in life when we may face hand to hand combat with the enemy. Sometimes we can feel as though we're alone fighting the enemy. Fear not, because we truly are never alone. Our General and Squad Leader are always overseeing. If we call on them in a time of need they will deliver us. There is never a moment when they will abandon us. So let's not abandon any one of our brothers or sisters serving with us. There are moments when one of our fellow troops may be hit and wounded by the enemy. It may appear that this person is running in and out of Holy consciousness. Whatever you do, do not give up on them. Don't leave them to die, try your best to resuscitate their spirit. The power of fellowship in our lives is miraculous and necessary. Although we personally may not be qualified to resuscitate the spirit of a brother or sister remember one thing: we are not alone. Our Lord promised that when two or more meet in His name, He will be present (Matthew 18:20). We may not always know what to do to help someone in pain, but our Almighty General and Squad Leader does. They are readily available whenever we speak their names. There are times when people we love are just going through it. It might feel as if they are impossible to deal with. Don't be so quick to dismiss them, be patient with them. If it gets to the point where you cannot be around them, there's one last thing we can resort to as their brother or sister: that is to simply pray for them. Never allow yourself to be so upset with them that you don't want to at least pray for them. Practice patience and resilience. Don't stop praying for them because they are acting in a way that doesn't please you. Imagine if God gave up on us every time we didn't act in a manner that pleases Him. We would be burning in Hell now. So, as sincerely as He saves us, let's attempt to save our people; at least through prayer. In life it is impossible for us to save a person who doesn't want to be saved. On the other hand, our God is powerful enough to save them. So surrender to our Almighty General through prayer and have faith that He will save your brother or sister.

In this army in which we fight there are many subgroups. These subgroups are divided. With the upcoming battle that we will fight, we need to stay strong and united. There is strength in numbers. Something that I never understood is why some different Christian denominations don't get along. If we are all under the same Christian army, then why are we separated? Not only are many people divided, but at times it appears that the groups sometimes downright hate each other. In these final days there is no time for us to have internal battles and friendly fire. Let's restore our relationships. At the end of the day we have faith in the same God, the same Jesus, and we refer to the same Bible. Some may read or interpret the word in different dialects, but it is nevertheless the same message. As long as we believe in the word of God and have a common enemy in the devil, why can't we put our differences aside? Why can't we fight alongside each other and not be against each other? By having this division and drama within fellow followers of Christ we are following the guidance of the enemy. Believe it or not, having this division is what the devil wants, not our Heavenly Father. Our Father and our Savior both stress the concept of loving everyone and being against anything evil. Nowhere does it mention that we should go against each other. Having this division among Christians is playing into the strategy of the devil. He wants us to be divided because he knows that there is strength in numbers. When we are divided, individually we are weaker. The enemy then feels that we are subject to be easy kills or held captive.

Think of it like this: Our enemy is similar to the big bully on the playground. Let's say that there are five Christians in the sandbox who are all average size. The five Christians are made up of different denominations. Alone the abnormally large bully might be able to defeat each average-sized individual one on one. But if all five Christians team up and ambush the bully, he can definitely be defeated. Each person can take out a leg, arm and his head. In the final days here on earth, let's think strategy, and let's unite.

The Uniform

In the book of Ephesians our uniform is described in detail. Everything that we are instructed to wear is designed to protect us from the enemy's attacks. We are also equipped with items designed to defeat our enemy in battle. Once we are dressed in our uniform it is important to understand who we are fighting. We must have an understanding that we are fighting against spirits and not people.

> *Put on the whole armor of God, that you may*
> *be able to stand against the wiles of the devil*
> *-Ephesians 6:11*

First we are instructed to put on the girded waist of truth. This specifically is our belt. Having this belt implies that we stay in the word of God with a humble open heart. From this, God can reveal where your heart is and help restore it if needed.

> *Therefore gird up the loins of your mind, be*
> *sober, and rest your hope fully upon the grace*
> *that is to be brought to you at the revelation*
> *of Jesus Christ. -1 Peter 1:13*

This helps us out because one of the enemy's favorite go-to weapons is deception. Being sound in the word of God serves as protection. This will keep God's truth with you at all times. In the world we live in, there are many preachers who will preach to you things that may not be Biblically correct. Don't just go to church and listen to an evangelist without doing your own research. Go to the word of God and see if their messages check out accurately. In the final days of this world there will be many false prophets. Some of these people may come off as really trustworthy individuals. They will deliver messages that may sound quite holy, but will be subtly off. As soldiers of God's army we must be able to detect the errors within these messages. One subtle lapse of judgment or deception could lead to our demise.

The uniform then calls for the breast plate of righteousness. Basically this means that we are doing what's morally correct through the laws of God. The breast plate itself serves as the part of the armor that shields vital organs such as the heart, lungs, etc. If we are hit in one of these organs we can be instantly killed physically and spiritually. This is displayed in Proverbs 11:4 where it says that *""Riches profit not in the day of wrath, but righteousness from death."*

Next, our feet should be shod in preparation of the Gospel of peace. This means that we should be ready to go to war whenever we are called to do so. We don't know when God may call us to go to battle, but we should be ready at all times with our shoes buckled. These shoes are important because they protect soldier's feet from harsh surfaces. The shoes will provide protection when walking on gravelly or rocky surfaces. The surface is symbolic of things that may lessen our performance for the Lord. Think of it this way: if you are running full speed and step on a nail, will you continue running at the same speed? Absolutely not! You performance will depreciate. We need our feet protected so we can keep taking steps in faith with the Lord.

This will also allow us to keep moving on the narrow path without slowing down even over harsh surfaces. It also allows us to keep up our pace when we are invading enemy territory. This section of the uniform also entails being prepared mentally.

> *But sanctify The Lord God in your hearts, and always be ready to give a defense to everyone who asks you a reason of the hope that is in you, with meekness and fear. 1 Peter 3:15*

With our shod feet we are also called to be prepared with the Gospel of Peace. This basically instructs us to spread peace across the world and to bear good fruit.

Our next part of our uniform is the Shield of Faith. We are supposed to hold this shield up when we are under attack. With this shield we are to deflect the darts and shots that the enemy fires at us. The enemy's favorite darts to throw are lies, deception, schemes and temptation. The goal is to get you to shift your focus away from God and put it toward something or someone else. If we are hit by one of these darts the wounds we can suffer are depression, doubt, desire to sin, hateful thoughts, and any thoughts of blasphemy. This is symbolic because in the human realm the shield protects the physical body; in the realm of faith, the shield protects the spiritual body of a soldier.

> *For by grace you have been saved through*
> *faith; and that not of yourselves: it is the gift*
> *of God. -Ephesians 2:8*

The next piece of the uniform is probably the most important. This one is the Helmet of Salvation. This helmet protects the soldier's head and mind during battle with the enemy. Then through salvation we are delivered by God from our sins. The deliverance occurs when we confess that Jesus is Lord and believe that God raised Him from death. We are then to turn away from sin and turn toward our Almighty General. From this point forward, we are viewed as being a new creation – also known as born again. Along with this process comes the renewal of our minds.

> *And do not be conformed to this world:*
> *but be transformed by the renewing of your*
> *mind, that you may prove what is that good*
> *and acceptable, and perfect will of God.*
> *-Romans 12:2*

The final part if the uniform is the Sword of Spirit. This sword is the word of a God and is more powerful than any weapon that our enemy carries. This weapon is used for up close, hand to hand combat. Some people refer to this as *Rhema*. In Greek, Rhema means "utterance" or "said thing." It's also defined as scripture that is spoken to a believer. This is the spoken word given to us by the Holy Spirit. These words serve as our hand to hand combat weapon while the enemy uses deception and lies.

11

MEET YOUR ENEMY

If you've made it this far in the book, you probably have noticed that every message has been delivered through a variation of a parable. Either it was a version of a parable or it had some metaphorical meaning. This will be the first and only chapter where that doesn't occur. Now I want to be as direct as possible. I don't want there to be any confusion about who our enemy is and what he's after. In fact, I feel that he would want me to use a creative little story to help lessen my message. That way the message would not be as bold or cutthroat. He wants me to show mercy on him. I could not care less what our enemy would like. I am writing this in honor of the army of the one and only true GOD. I am a child of God and He sent His only begotten son to die on the cross for my sins (John 3:16). For that I can never repay Him, but I will absolutely try my best. With that in mind, this chapter is meant to expose our enemy. I'm writing this chapter as a way of stepping on the enemy's neck and snapping it. In the book of Luke (Luke10:19), Jesus gives us the authority to trample over the enemy. And I am going to do just that. Our enemy is very aware of my intent in this chapter. He will do any and everything in his power to make sure this message isn't delivered or comprehended. You can, therefore, definitely expect him to intervene and attempt to take you away from this message. But through the grace of God, I have faith that this message will resonate with all of its readers. Before we get into the actual message, I would like everyone to read this prayer that I have prepared.

> *Dear Heavenly Father,*
>
> *I humbly and graciously bow down before you with aspirations of bringing glory to your name. Heavenly Father, I thank you for who you are and who you have made me. Lord, I pray that you watch over and bless any eyes that may scan these pages. May every single word in this chapter be blessed, anointed, and correspond with your Word in the name of Jesus. Please remove any impurities that possibly may have been written. May your glory shine through any gaps or holes that may be present. I pray that you guide and direct us. Then please shield and protect us from any evil or demonic spirits*

that may approach us during this chapter. I know that our enemy will try everything to diminish this chapter. But, Lord, I have faith that through you, our Kingdom will be victorious with this message. In Revelation 12:9 it's says that our enemy was cast down to the earth with his followers. Lord I am here to share and remind every reader of the message of John 4:4. It says, "He who is in you is greater than he who is in the World." So therefore I want everyone to know that with you it's impossible for us to be defeated. I pray for the removal of any fear or doubt that may lie within one's heart while reading this. With you, God, we can accomplish anything and apart from you we can do nothing. Thank you for your love, grace, patience and forgiveness. Without you I am nothing and without you I am no one. Please bless these words and message.

In Jesus Christ's name I pray. Amen!

The first thing that I want everyone to realize is that with our enemy there is nothing to fear. I know this topic may very well scare many people and that's what he wants it to do. I feel that the fear that some people have about our enemy comes from a lack of knowledge. Through this chapter I plan to provide everyone with the knowledge needed to overcome any fear that may reside in them. The enemy wants us to believe that ignorance is bliss. In actuality, this very ignorance strengthens the enemy and leads to our demise. The way I see it, he knows everything about us and knows how to attack us. So we should know everything about him, how to attack him, and how to protect ourselves.

So who exactly is our enemy? He goes by many names and I will list a few: he is referred to as the devil, Lucifer, Satan, and so on. In the Bible you may see him referred to as the serpent, the prince of air, king of tyre, son of morning, and so forth.

So where did he come from and how did he get here?

Our enemy was initially a creation of God, who was given the name of Lucifer. Lucifer was one of God's three Arch Angels along with Gabriel (Messenger), and Michael (Protector/Leader in War). In Heaven, Lucifer was in charge of worship and was the Heavenly Song Leader. He was actually one of God's most cherished Angels. He was made perfect in beauty and was filled with wisdom. He was the most beautiful Angel.

> *You were the seal of perfection, Full of wisdom and perfect in beauty. You were in Eden, the garden of God; Every precious stone was your covering: The sardius, topaz, and diamond, Beryl, onyx, and jasper, sapphire, turquoise, and emerald with gold. The workmanship of*

your timbrels and pipes was prepared for you
on the day you were created. -Ezekiel 28:13

He was even anointed to be in the presence of The
Lord and to cover the mountain of God.

You were the anointed cherub (winged angelic
being) who covers; I established you; you were
on the Holy Mountain of God; you walked
back and forth in the midst of fiery stones.
You were perfect in your ways from the day
you were created. -Ezekiel 28:14-15

So how did this prized Angel fall from grace?

Lucifer fell from grace by becoming prideful, im-
moral, violent and arrogant. Because he was extremely
blessed by God and held in such a high regard, he became arrogant. He saw that he was held higher above
all of the other angels and let it go to his head (Ezekiel
28:15-17). He began to think that he was greater than
God. This was when everything that he once stood for
became corrupt. He felt as though he could be God
and that he could run things (Isaiah 14:13-15). When
that happened, God had Lucifer kicked out of Heaven.

You were perfect in your ways from the day you
were created. Till iniquity was found in you.
By the abundance of your trading you became
filled with violence within, and you sinned;

Therefore I cast you as a profane thing out of the mountain of God; and I destroyed you, O covering cherub, from the midst of the fiery stones. Your heart was lifted up because of your beauty; You corrupted your wisdom for the sake of your splendor. I cast you to the ground, I laid you before kings, that they might gaze at you. -Ezekiel 28:15-17

For you have said in your heart: I will ascend into Heaven, I will exalt my throne above the stars of God; I will also sit on the mount of the congregation on the farthest sides of the North, I will ascend above the heights of the clouds, I will be like the Most High.' Yet you shall be brought down to Sheol, To the lowest depths of the pit. -Isaiah 14:13-15

Lucifer was then sent to earth. In Ezekiel it says that God had already destroyed Lucifer. Then in the book of Matthew, it says that God had prepared an everlasting fire for the devil and his Angel (Matthew 25:41). The devil at one time was the Angel who was closest to God. He led the worship in Heaven. Therefore he knew that God would fulfill all His promises and he knew that God has the ultimate power. So right now he is counting down the days he has until he burns in Hell for Eternity (Revelation 12:12). Since he's already screwed up his citizenship in the Kingdom of

God, he's looking to make others do the same. He doesn't want to burn in the fiery pits of Hell alone. This was even displayed back when he was thrown out of Heaven. It's said that when he fell from Heaven so did one-third of the angels (Revelation 12:4, Revelation 12:9). Now that he is out Heaven, he knows what's coming next. He knows that when Jesus Christ returns he will be kicked out of Earth and sent to Hell. So his goal during this time period is to get as many people as possible to go with him. The idea of this scares many people, when it really shouldn't. Fear only resides in the people who lack knowledge on this topic. I would like to encourage everyone who fears this topic to really learn the word of God. Read His word in the Bible, pray to Him nonstop, and meditate. The more knowledge you have the better off you will be. In this case knowledge is power and ignorance will lead to your demise. The strength of knowledge is shown throughout the Bible in places like Proverbs 1:5 where it says that "a man of understanding will attain wise counsel. It then goes on to say in line 7 that "The fear of 'The Lord' is the beginning of knowledge." Notice how it says the fear of "The Lord" not the devil. So therefore why would we even fear this coward called the devil. In the book of Ephesians we are called to take the Sword of the Spirit, which is the word of God. This basically says that we are supposed to fight the devil and defeat him by using the word of God. So how can we possibly defeat the devil if we are not knowledgeable on God's word? At times I like to refer to the enemy as the king of misery. As the old cliché says, "Misery loves company." This is especially true regarding Satan. He doesn't want to go Hell alone; he wants others to go with him. He knows that if we are not knowledgeable on the word of God, we will be more vulnerable to his attacks. The vulnerability that we display may possibly then lead to our joining him in Hell. I can't stress this enough, please become knowledgeable on the word of God. Knowledge is Power. Below I am going to list off some things that the devil doesn't want you to know. If you aren't knowledgeable about the following items, the enemy will most likely attack you in these areas.

What the enemy doesn't want you to know!!!

1.) *God The Father is real! God the Son is real! God the Holy Spirit is real!*
2.) *The devil is real!*
3.) *Heaven is real! Hell is real!*
4.) *Angels are real! Demons and Evil Spirits are real!*
5.) *Jesus died on the cross for our sins so that we could be forgiven for our sins and still go to Heaven for eternity.*
6.) *Jesus rose from the dead and will return to earth for the rest of God's Children.*
7.) *God is forgiving and will forgive us as long as we repent (Acts 3:19).*

8.) *You cannot deny Jesus and get into Heaven (1 John 2:23).*

9.) *We cannot do anything without God (John 15:5).*

10.) *The devil has already been defeated (Ezekiel 28:15-17).*

11.) *We have more power than the devil (Luke 10:19).*

12.) *There will come a day where every knee will bow down to God and every tongue will confess that Jesus is Lord (Romans 14:11), (Philippians 2:10).*

13.) *Blasphemy against the Holy Spirit is the only sin that cannot be forgiven (Matthew 12:31,32) (Mark 3:28-30).*

These are just some of the things that our enemy doesn't want us know. And there are certainly more. Again, I say knowledge is power!

Next I would like to share with you tactics that the enemy may use to attack you. Through these tactics he wants to change our minds and beliefs. He wants to try to get us to think differently and view things in a way that goes against the morals of God. That's why it's important to protect our minds. That's why in Ephesians we are instructed to take the Helmet of Salvation and the Sword of Spirit at the same time. It shields us from the enemy's tactics and helps us fight back. Truthfully the devil possibly knows the word of God better than many of us. Let's not forget that he led worship on the highest scale. Through this next part, I want to share with you some of his tactics. These tactics are lies, deception, fear, anger, hatred, confusion, temptation and more. Through these tactics he hopes to reel you into depression, oppression and possession. If he is able to put you into any of these three states of mind, he knows you will be much more vulnerable to his attacks.

Lies and Deception

Some of Satan's most effective tactics are his lies and deception. This is something that he has done since the beginning of mankind. He lied to Adam and Eve. He told them that if they ate the fruit they would be like God. He then convinced them into thinking that God was withholding certain things from them. I would like to also let people know that his lies are not just a thing of the past. He still uses this tactic on a daily basis. If you are not knowledgeable about the word of God, he'll do the same to you. He will plant things in your head that are complete lies. With these lies he hopes to reel you into depression, oppression, and possession. He wants you to obtain these traits, but at this point you are a bigger target to hit. He will plant things in your head that completely contradict God's word. The devil wants to make you think that certain things come from God when they really come from him. With every thought that enters your brain, it's important to ask yourself: Is this of God or the enemy? Understand that the two are complete opposites and could never coexist.

The devil also likes to place emphasis on fear. He wants us to be afraid of him. In that regard the devil is like the bully on the playground. Bullies are truly cowards at heart. Through research I discovered that bullies are looking to be in control or obtain a sense of authority. They also like to pick on people who cannot defend themselves or whom they perceive as weak. Does this sound familiar? In Isaiah, Satan said that he would exalt his throne above the stars of God's. By that he means that he wants to be in control and would like God's authority. He then attempts to find people who can't defend themselves or may not know how to defend themselves. Then, like most bullies, he continues to pick on those individuals. As with most bullies, when we stand up to them we find out just how weak they actually are. Learning the word of God is truly self-defense against our enemy. With acquired self-defense we can defeat this bully every single time.

Another thing the devil will try to use is hatred and anger. He knows that God calls for us to be joyful, loving and caring. So expect the devil to try to provoke you in many ways. He may use the person whom you dislike at work, maybe your significant other, maybe your friends, or your family. In this scenario we must stand strong to our faith. We must learn to acknowledge that it is our enemy working through these people. We are battling against spirits not the people themselves. Sad to say some people don't realize that they are being used by the devil to get under your skin. As followers of Christ, we must be sure not to let the devil use us as well. We shouldn't provoke others looking for an angry response. The only emotions that we should ever look to bring out of others is happiness and love.

Next there is confusion. This is a tactic that the enemy often loves to use. Confusion is definitely something that isn't from our God. If there is one thing He's not, it's confusing. When you read the Bible, you notice that God is very straightforward. You never see him giving unclear directions to anyone; He is and was always very direct. When He gave insight to Adam, Eve, Moses, Job, and others, He was very specific about what he wanted. When any Biblical people disappointed Him, He made it clear how He felt and showed His wrath if needed. At no point in the Bible were any individuals left for any period of time wondering how God felt. Because of that, you can assume that confusion usually comes from the enemy. If you diligently seek God when you're at a place in life where you are confused about your placement, I promise He will end that confusion for you.

One of the final tactics that I'd like to address is temptation. The enemy loves to tempt you with things and people that are detrimental to you. He knows you very well so he will use things that you desire to tempt you, especially if it's something unholy. If you have addictions, expect for temptation to come in that form. When you try to change for the better, expect to feel an urge to return to the previous ways. Expect people from your problem period to reenter your life. To sum up, always remember Satan will tempt you through temptation of the eyes, flesh and pride of life (1 John 2:15-18).

I remember a time in my life when I really wasn't too knowledgeable on the word of God. I feel as though the devil sent some people to deceive me. I will never forget this day, it was in December of 2010, just a couple of weeks before Christmas. I was working as a waiter at a well-known corporate restaurant. On this day I waited on a married couple. Our conversation started off very normal – order taking, and entree delivering. But our normal conversational exchange was to take a dramatic turn. Near the end of their dinner, they both looked at me and told me that I was one of the chosen ones.

In my head I was thinking, "What *are these people talking about?*" Naturally, I arrogantly thought that they were referring to the service I had just given them. So I conceitedly responded, "Of course, well you know, I try my best."

Their response was, "No, really, you are one of the chosen ones!" They asked if I believed in God.

"Yes, I sure do!" I said.

The husband then said, "Hey, you're one of us." They explained, "We were called by God to find His other children. Children who are also 'chosen.'" They asked my age and I told them I was twenty years old. "When's your birthday?" The husband asked and I responded

"May 25th," I said.

The husband then said, "I'm sorry to inform you, but you will not see your twenty-first birthday. This will also be your last Christmas holiday coming up."

I was thinking, "*Okay, these people are definitely psychopaths. Did this guy just deliver a death threat to me?*" During these days I wasn't as disciplined in my faith. So I tensed up, and clenched my fist. I ultimately prepared myself for the unexpected. The guy looked at my face and said, "No, No, you are one of us, our job is to help alert and prepare our brothers and sisters for the end of world." He handed me a brochure that stated how the world would end on May 20th the following year. He said that through numbers used in the Bible, the world was subject to end on the given date. I wasn't completely sold on this idea, but I was filled with uncertainty. I was slightly confused. The idea of the world possibly ending at that time scared me. At that moment I knew one thing for sure: I needed God more than ever. I took the brochure and took their check off of the table. I walked away for no more than a minute to cash their bill out. To my surprise, when I returned to the table they had vanished. This was definitely peculiar because I only left the table for a minute. Besides, for them to have left the restaurant, they would have had to walk past me. Their disappearance only added to my confusion. Who were these people? How did they know about my faith? Were they really sent by God? Will the earth soon as they said?

Later that evening I went home and asked my mother if she knew that the earth might end soon. Loosely paraphrasing, her response was, "It may end soon! It may not! No one knows for sure when the world will end except God himself." She pointed me towards Matthew 24:36 which says that no one but God the Father knows the hour and day. No angels know when the world will end. More important, not even Jesus knows when He will return and end this world. If not even Jesus knows the end, how could some random person off the street know? Again, I want to emphasize that knowledge is power! In this situation, I witnessed all the devil's tactics. The couple *lied and deceived* me into believing that the world would end soon. There was a moment when I almost became *angry* at the guy for saying that I wouldn't see my next birthday. After that, I left and was extremely confused. I want to stress that every last one of these emotions are traits and tactics of the devil. These things are the complete opposite of God. It's important for us children to be able to draw parallels and notice the contradictions in our lives. We must be able to identify what is of God and what is of the enemy. Remember everything about the enemy is the complete opposite of God.

Contradictions
Devil says: You're ugly and your image isn't correct
God says: I made you to my likeness

> *God created man in His own image; in the image of God He created him. -Genesis 1:27*

Devil: Brings on feelings of hatred and anger
God: Brings happiness and says we should be joyful and love others

> *Rejoice in The Lord always. Again I will say rejoice! -Philippians 4:4*

> *You shall love you neighbor as yourself -Mark 12:31*

Devil: Brings arrogance and wants people to be prideful
God: Calls for us to be humble

> *Therefore humble yourselves under the mighty hand of God, that He may exalt you in due time, casting all your care upon Him, for He cares for you.   -1 Peter 5:6*

Devil: Fills you with the emotion of greed
God: Wants us to be generous

> *But this I say: He sows sparingly will also reap sparingly, and he who sows bountifully will also reap bountifully. So let's each one give as he purposes in his heart, not grudgingly or of necessity; for God loves a cheerful giver. -2 Corinthian 9:6,7*

Devil: Brings you doubt and causes you to worry
God: Wants you to have faith

> *Assuredly, I say to you, if you have faith and*
> *do not doubt, you will not only do what was*
> *done to the fig tree, but also if you say to this*
> *mountain, be removed and be cast into the*
> *sea, it will be done. And whatever things you*
> *ask in prayer, believing, You will receive.*
> *-Matthew 21:21*

Devil: Encourages you to fornicate
God: Encourages you to wait until marriage and for-
bids adultery

> *Flee sexual immorality. Every sin that a man*
> *does is outside the body, but he who commits*
> *sexual immorality sins against his own body.*
> *-1 Corinthians 6:18*

> *Whoever commits adultery with a woman*
> *lacks understanding; He who does so destroys*
> *his own soul.   -Proverbs 6:32*

Devil: Brings you confusion and encourages your
ignorance
God: Wants you to be knowledgeable and wise

Wisdom is the principal thing; therefore get wisdom. And in all your getting, get understanding. Exhalt her, and she will promote you; she will bring you honor, when you embrace her.   -Proverbs 4:6-7

<u>When and Why he Attacks</u>

The devil attacks people because he doesn't want us to get close to God. The enemy is an outcast and wants us all to join him. He doesn't want us receiving the relationship that he lost with God. There are some major times when you will notice him attack you. First is when you decide to commit yourself to The Lord or when you're trying to get closer. The enemy doesn't want to see anyone help strengthen the Kingdom of God. Sometimes I think this guy is delusional, psychotic, or just plain stupid. Actually, Satan is all three. He is afraid of God's army getting any stronger – as if he can stop it. He knows that his days are numbered, so he's attempting to create as much havoc as possible.

He attacks when God has a tremendous blessing in store for you and also when you're already blessed. The enemy is seeking to steal your blessing and glory.

Another time he will attack you is when you're attempting to expose him. I am definitely a living testament to this. The devil attacked very hard during the process of writing this book. He used everything, from temptation, distractions, procrastination, doubt, and we even had spiritual warfare in a dream I will share a little later. Satan also viciously attacks when you're trying to break out of a habitual sin or an unholy relationship. At this moment he will plant things in your head and try to convince you that you're doing the wrong thing. He will try to send you a ridiculous amount of temptation as well. Luckily for us, God will never allow us to be overwhelmingly tempted.

> *No temptation has overtaken you except such as is common to man; but God is faithful, who will not allow you to be tempted beyond what you are able, but with the temptation will also make the way of escape, that you may be able to bear it.* - *1 Corinthians 10:13*

The Ways he Attacks

Physically: There are times when he may use illness or injury to try to shake your faith. In these situations he will either try to get you to question God, or prevent you from doing something that God would like you to do.

Mentally: He will attack your mind. He will throw doubt, deception, and unrighteous things in your head. He will play mind tricks on you that will make the things in your life "too loud." He will try to make your life so loud that The Lord's voice will be drowned out or distorted. Here's when your judgment may become altered. When I refer to your life being loud, I'm not saying it in reference to sound.

The term is referring to the things that are going on in your life. So the loud sound could be your unnecessarily busy schedule, a stressed-out relationship, peer pressure, abuse, addictions, and so forth. These are things that may take time or mental attention away from God.

Spiritually: It's very possible that there's a demon spirit that arises in you at various times. The devil has done thorough research on you and knows you well. He definitely knows what your flaws are so he will send demonic spirits that specialize in those flaws. It's like when people say, "I guess they never conquered their demons...I battled with my demons for a long time." It's not just an old expression people use. It really means just that. Think about it: when you are intoxicated, your mind goes to another place. That place is with that demon. You begin to act in a way that you normally wouldn't. There are also those situations for people with anger issues. When some people get past their breaking point, they may snap. They say things that are meant to hurt others. In some cases they get violent attack, and at the point of attack, they lose their sanity. The same is true for addictions, gambling, drugs, sexuality, drinking and so on. With addictions, you have that thing that triggers you (temptation sent by the devil). For instance even when you're trying to quit, you convince yourself that you have the willpower not to overdo it. But that never works. Once you give in to that trigger, you become engulfed by that addiction. This is where the spirit begins to control you.

My Personal Spiritual Attack

During the process of writing this book, the enemy definitely tried to attack. One of the most memorable attacks came to me within a dream. In this dream I had to take part in spiritual warfare. The dream started with me being a spectator at an out of town at an event. The event I attended was a conference that had multiple sessions. At this conference there were a couple of ushers that I met and came to know. After the event, as I was leaving, I shook hands with one usher that I'd gotten to know. We said farewell and he wished me well on my endeavors. In this dream the main endeavor that he referred to was this book. I then shook hands with the second usher. This second one was a small guy who had a deformed hand that bent in an awkward direction. I just remember I felt so bad for him because of his deformity.

When I was saying goodbye to him, I shook his hand using my right hand. We could both see that my grip was slightly stronger than his.

He said to me, jokingly, "Hey, I'm disabled man; you have to shake with your left hand so I can have a professional, strong grip."

I looked at him. I was thinking how much I really didn't want to do that. In the dream I didn't want to do that for a couple of reasons. The truth is I was disgusted by his hand and I was always taught to shake with my right hand. But I felt badly for him and didn't want to offend him. And I felt guilty. So I went ahead and shook his hand using my left hand. He chose to shake with his right, deformed hand. His deformity bend his hand in the opposite direction so that it aligned perfectly with my left hand. We clenched and shook hands. I noticed his right hand gaining a ridiculous amount of strength. He was really squeezing my hand very hard, to the point where it started to hurt. As his grip got stronger, I noticed his hand was becoming darker. The color shifted from his wrist toward the tips of fingers. It was as if his blood was rushing to the tips of his fingers.

As the blood of his hand began to reach his fingertips, he looked me in the eyes and said, "Unleash the beast." The moment he said that, for some reason, I thought about my book. I began to forget everything I'd written to that point, and all the ideas I still had for it. Within a short time I began to forget everything about Christianity, and I began to forget about God. The usher's thoughts had been placed in my head and he wanted me to destroy God's Kingdom. In that moment in my dream I was angry at God. Then something in my head told me not to let his blood reach his fingertips. I somehow knew that if that occurred, I would be on his side. At the very last second, I shouted, "I bleed the blood of Jesus!"

As soon as I'd said it, his grip immediately got weaker. I said it a second time. "I bleed the blood of Jesus!" This time something interesting happened. This time I not only said it in my dream but also in real life. The second time I said, "I bleed the blood of Jesus," I was actually awake in my bedroom. Upon waking, I noticed that my hand was numb and had no feeling in it. I sat up and wept for at least fifteen minutes. During those fifteen minutes I experienced an array of emotions. I was *grateful* that God saved me and honestly saved my soul. I felt *comfort* knowing that by just saying the name, Jesus, I scared the devil off. I felt more *love* for God than ever, and I knew that I never wanted to lose that feeling. I felt *offended* by the devil and his attempt to convert me. And I felt *angry* at him for trying to get me to go against Jesus. The Holy Spirit instructed me to use this aggression against the devil. Once I received this message, I felt very powerful and was ready to go to war against the devil. At that moment I vowed to solely work for God and to empower God's Kingdom.

HOW TO DEFEAT THE ENEMY

There are quite a few ways to defeat the enemy in possible battles. These are:

1) By living a holy and righteous life

2) By knowing who you are in Christ

(You are a child of God. Through the grace of God we have been redeemed by the blood of

Christ. You have been forgiven for your sins, and are sealed with the Holy Spirit)

3) Through the Holy Spirit we are blessed with discernment. With this we must be able to recognize when demonic influences may be the cause

4) Recite number 2 out loud. This time make it in first person narrative. *(Using "I" and "My")*

(I am a child of God. Through the grace of God I have been redeemed by the blood of Christ. I have been forgiven for my sins and I am sealed with the Holy Spirit)

5) State your power and authority over the enemy. Then in Jesus's name, command the demonic and evil spirits to leave your presence

This is an example of verbal spiritual warfare defense. This is only one of many variations.

"Demonic and evil spirits, I stand here against you in the name of Jesus Christ. I am drenched in the blood of Jesus. I am a Child of God. At this moment I demand that you

leave my presence and you leave me alone. In Jesus's name! In Jesus's name! In Jesus's name! In Jesus Christ's name!"

MODERN DAY PRESENCE

How does the enemy impact the modern world? There are many ways that our enemy impacts our modern world. For the average person, most of what our enemy does goes undetected. But with the proper knowledge, we can identify the works of the enemy and cast them down. The first method of identifying his works is by completely knowing him. What is his appearance like? What are his characteristics? Why was he kicked out of Heaven? By knowing the answers to these three questions alone you will be able to notice parallels between those answers and everyday society.

First let's examine his appearance, as described in the Bible.

You were the seal of perfection, Full of wisdom and perfect in beauty. You were in Eden, the garden of God; Every precious stone was your covering. The sardius, topaz, and diamond, beryl, onyx, and jasper, sapphire, turquoise, and emerald with gold. The workmanship of your timbrels and pipes was prepared for you on the day you were created. -Ezekiel 28:13

From this scripture alone we learn that he was perfect in appearance and was covered in precious jewels. He had timbrels and pipes, which are musical instruments. These are all things that he acquired from God before he was kicked out of Heaven. When he became arrogant, these were some of the things he valued. These exact things are what he felt made him important. Therefore it's possible that he applies these attributes to impact the world. Now that we have this knowledge, let's look at society today. In the world today the easiest way to reach the masses is through television, film, music, media outlets, advertisements, and so forth. In most of these industries there is a heavy emphasis placed upon appearance. The society we live in says that we must live up to the standards of these "sex symbols." Society says that if we don't have the perfect body, skin, hair, etc., we are lacking. In every advertisement these people look flawless. Their images are plastered everywhere; on billboards, social media, magazines, television, etc. These images deliver a false message of importance. In everyday society there are many who will attempt to imitate these images. The ones who are able to mimic their appearance best are thought to be superior to others. Because of this attitude, people who don't measure up are picked on in school and looked down on – in this situation, they might very likely develop low self-esteem, and depression. Because Lucifer had a perfect appearance, he tries to convince all of us that we should value image over morals. Think about it: one of the devil's tactics, "Lust of the eyes" only works if an appealing image is portrayed.

The devil will also sometimes send people that you find attractive to be in a relationship with you. If these people are devil sent, they usually bring a lot of stress into your life. They will cause you to do things against the Will of God. For this reason, he is going to work hard to send you someone who sparks your interest. He'll send you someone who will be able to get you to lower your guard.

Think about it. These images of perfect men and women are pounded into our heads starting at an early age. And the repetition of these values serves to embed these ideas in our heads. We want to be like the perfect people we've been conditioned to admire, and we look for that in real life. The people who don't meet the standards of these images become outcasts. Once they become outcasts, they are often overlooked by the opposite sex. After being overlooked so many times, a sense of doubt grows in them. They begin to feel as if something is wrong with them. These feelings can bring on depression, doubt, and even suicidal thoughts. Let's reiterate the fact that one of the enemy's goals is to kill. At the point of depression (killing spirit) and suicide (killing body) he is doing just that. He will try to get you to kill yourself because he wants you to ruin the plans that God has for you. If he can get you to do this before repenting, he knows that there is a chance that you will join him in hell. Remember that he was originally created beautiful with precious stones, so a lot emphasis is placed on beauty. People believe that their appearance determines their status in society. They feel that acquiring cars, designer clothes, and jewelry will deliver a sense of wealth. I want to tell you that true wealth is acquired through your spirit and mind, not from material things. It seems that most people are overly worried about the image they portray. If you look at impoverished inner cities there are many people who are disappointed with their living conditions. Some people in these conditions believe that there is a correlation between their impoverished living conditions and their happiness. While living in these conditions they view wealthy people in the media as being happy. When they put these two ideas together, they begin to believe that these wealthy people are happy because of the materials that they acquired. In actuality, this is far from the truth. When a person living in poverty adopts this mentality the devil is able to work through them. He is able to convince them that if they acquire material items they will receive glory. That is why you see many people in the inner city walking around with expensive things. They want to be like the people in the media. What's ironic about their situation is that the people in the media are being used solely to manipulate viewers. They are able to use their platform to influence the masses. In these magazines, music videos, commercials, you see these people with luxury items. It seems as if they are living great lives and are desired by everyone. In reality, many of these people have material wealth and still lack happiness. They realize that it's not all that it's cracked up to be. These material items will never accrue spiritual wealth. The jewels themselves are not evil, God created those. He wouldn't mind His people acquiring them if it were in His will. If you think about it, Heaven actually has streets paved with gold, and things made of precious stones. So the jewels and luxurious items are not evil themselves. What's evil is how people make these items the center of their lives. When that happens, these items become idols, which God dislikes (there's a commandment against this). People let these material items, along with money, run their lives. For some people it becomes an obsession. In the pursuit of this kind of material wealth, people fulfill the devil's goal. They commit crimes of burglary, robbery, embezzlement (they steal). There are people who kill others who get in the way of their obtaining these material items (kill). There have been instances where people were killed waiting in line for sneakers. There are examples where people have killed in revenge on the person who stole from them. There are people who let material items alter their better judgment. There are people who will buy jewels and clothing before providing for their own children, ultimately destroying their lives, psyches, and communities (destroy).

Next examine how the enemy had instruments built in him. When he was in Heaven, he was in charge of worship. And Satan is very knowledgeable of the power of music. He knows that a single song that is played over and over can impact millions of people all at once. So there are many catchy songs that people love to sing along with. People may very well be singing along to a song that goes against the word of God. Such songs might encourage fornication, adultery, violence, hatred, etc. The power of music and sound is truly astonishing. The power of music and sound is shown in the Bible with the stories of Joshua and David. In the story of Joshua, he was instructed by God to circle the city walls while playing music. After doing so, the walls of Jericho fell and they were able to take over the city (Joshua 6:4,5). Then there's the example of David who played the harp in before King Saul. At the time, King Saul was oppressed by an evil spirit that resided within him. Astonishingly, every time David played the harp, the evil spirit would leave the king (1 Samuel 16:23).

The devil also works through entertainment such as film, TV, and video games. These things are used to give visual examples of how the devil wants us to live. In the past there used to be TV shows on the major networks that portrayed great morals. Those have been replaced by reality shows, sitcoms, and other shows that contradict everything God wants. On these shows you see things like excessive anger, sex, violence, and so forth. Unfortunately, TV is overly saturated with these types of shows. These kinds of shows vastly outnumber shows that have good morals. The shows with the morals are usually only shown on channels that people hardly watch.

Modern Day Influences

In modern day America there are many symbols or figures that people take part in. Sometimes people don't realize that these things are against God. For example, such things would include mediums, Ouija boards, tarot card readings, magic ball readings, witchcraft, zombies, etc. As children of God, we shouldn't support any of these things in any way, shape, or form. God strongly dislikes seeing us take part in any of these activities. Sometimes society will try to convince us that these things are just harmless fun. To people of the world it may very well be, but we are not of this world. We belong to the Kingdom of God and are held to a higher standard. I also want to stress that these things are not harmless. By taking part in these things we are inviting evil demonic spirits into our presence. Once these demonic spirits arrive, the devil is capable of working within our lives. Take mediums and spiritualists, for example. These people like to take advantage of individuals who are in a vulnerable mental state. These are usually people who are lost spiritually or are looking for some sort of closure with respect to a loved one who has passed away. In this state of mind, these people try to lean on their own understanding. Obviously, they fail miserably in their attempts. They go to these mediums or spiritualists to help them solve their problems. This is absolutely the wrong way to find what you're looking for. I am here to tell you that the only way to get your closure is through Jesus Christ. He is the only way! Never resort to any other method to find your solution. These mediums are certainly the works of the devil. He wants you to think there are ways to solve your issues other than through God. Always remember that the devil is a liar. God is the only way! The devil is a fraud and the ultimate deceiver. These mediums and spiritualists want you to believe that they really are connecting with your loved one who passed away. I'm going to tell you that they are talking to spirits directly, but not the spirits you think. They are talking directly to demonic spirits who are manipulating you in your vulnerable state. These people are cowards, liars, and deceivers. They want you to think that your loved one is sending you a message, when it's really the devil who knows your background story and delivers it to that medium. So because they are telling you things you thought were private, you begin to trust them as a credible source. You begin to believe that they are telling the truth. Once they have your trust, they are able to plant things in your head that go against the ways of the Kingdom of God. I can't stress to you how dangerous these interactions can be. Understand that we are children of God and we are called to resist the devil. Let's not make it easy for him to attack us by welcoming him into our presence through his deception. Let's remember that knowledge is power. We must really ask ourselves a question: why would we ever contemplate depending on these spiritualists or mediums? These people are frauds. All they are doing is calling on random spirits to give you answers. Why would you waste your time and money dealing with these people, when we already have the ultimate spirit within us? The spirit that we have within us is the Holy Spirit. With this Holy Spirit we have access to any answers we need. So why would we ever pay these frauds your hard earned money to contact their fraudulent and demonic spirits when we have the Holy Spirit living within us for free? Meanwhile these demon-filled spiritualists will say that they can connect you with a spirit for "$.99 a minute." (Just as an example.) God comes to live inside you, providing you with the Holy Spirit for absolutely FREE. The Holy Spirit that lives within us has already been purchased for us through the blood of Jesus Christ.

Finally, I want to stress that by reaching out to these mediums, we are denying God. The people who provide these fake answers and those who seek them are really saying that God's answers, which lie within us, are not good enough. The message is that we can't trust the spirit that God gave us. I truly feel sorry for people who don't trust the Holy Spirit. If you don't trust the Holy Spirit, then then you don't truly know the Holy Spirit. If you don't know the Holy Spirit, you don't know yourself!

> *When you come into the land which the Lord*
> *your God is giving you, you shall not learn to*

> *follow the abominations of those nations. There shall not be found among you anyone who makes his son or his daughter pass through the fire, or one who practices witchcraft, or a soothsayer, or one who interprets omens, or a sorcerer, or one who conjures spells, or a medium, or a spiritist, or one who calls up the dead. For all who do these things are an abomination to the Lord, and because of these abominations the Lord your God drives them out from before you. - Deuteronomy 18:9-12*

The Anti-Christ

The Bible says that in the final days there will come a man known as the Anti-Christ. He will be a very deceptive individual. He might be seen as highly charismatic and will be loved by many people. Once he has power and control, he will try to influence the world with ideas that are against the word of God. He will try to deceive many Christians and try to get them to adopt inaccurate philosophies. He will attempt to mark humans with something known as the "Mark of the Beast." During this time period, many Christians will be persecuted and die for their faith in God. I want to encourage you not to be afraid because we are not of this world. If we die here on earth, we will definitely wake up and rise again in the paradise known as Heaven. Let the people of this world fear death because they are the ones unsure about where they are going afterward. As followers of Jesus Christ, let's be confident and stand tall in our faith. In our afterlife we will be sent to paradise where there is only happiness, great health and love.

> *Little children, it is the last hour; and as you have heard that the Antichrist is coming, even now many antichrist have come, by which we know that it is the last hour. -1 John 2:18*

> *Who is a liar but he who denies that Jesus is the Christ? He is antichrist who denies the Father and the Son. Whoever denies the Son does not have the Father either; he who acknowledges the Son has the Father also. -1 John 2:22*

> *And every spirit that does not confess that Jesus Christ has come in the flesh is not of God. And this is the spirit of the Antichrist, which you have heard was coming, and is now already in the world. -1 John 4:3*

> *For many deceivers have gone out into the world who do not confess Jesus Christ as coming in the flesh. This is a deceiver and an antichrist. -2 John 7*

And he was given a mouth speaking great things and blasphemies, and he was given authority to continue for forty-two months.

Then he opened his mouth in blasphemy against a God to blaspheme His name, His tabernacle, and those who dwell in Heaven

It was granted to him to make war with saints and to overcome them. And authority was given him over every tribe, tongue, and nation.

All who dwell on the Earth will worship him, whose names have not been written in the book of life of the lamb slain from the foundation of the world. -Revelations 13:5-8

12

THE CLIFFHANGER

ey, Dad, I'm glad you woke me up because I just had the craziest dream ever. In my dream, my day started off like any other day. I began it by running on this mountain top. For some reason the more I ran, the more speed I picked up. It got to the point where I couldn't slow down. I just kept running and running. Then it came to a point where I noticed that the mountain was coming to an end. I felt my heart gyrate at an unbelievably fast rate. It was as if there were some living creature being tortured in my heart and it was trying its best to escape. My nerves were unreal at this moment. As I began to approach the edge of the cliff, my mind wanted me to stop running, but my heart wouldn't allow me. I had to make a decision. I could run off the cliff, fall to my death, or attempt to grab ahold of something. As I took my last step off of the cliff, I tried to reach for this rock. I was able to grab the rock with both hands, but I quickly lost my grip. Because of the amount of force pulling me from the opposite direction, I kept sliding toward the edge of the cliff. As this overwhelming force dragged my body off of the cliff, I tried to sink my fingers into the ground, but I failed tremendously. I frantically fought to grab hold of something, anything! I desperately needed my life saved. I fell off the cliff. As I tumbled down, I made one last effort to save my life. I swung my arms over my head and was able to grab the very edge of the mountain. The gritty surface of the cliff pierced my hands, making it almost unbearable to keep my grip on the mountain. The piercing hurt so much that I actually contemplated just taking my chances and falling. That idea soon vanished when I saw what awaited me down below. It was at least a 100-foot drop – one I could definitely not survive. Honestly the 100-foot drop was the least of my worries. I looked down and saw my feet dangling over a boisterous pit of fire. The flames in the pit swayed from left to right, leaping over one another like gazelles in the Sahara attempting to escape a predator. In addition to that, there were gusty winds strong enough to put the most treacherous tornado to shame, ultimately causing the flames to expand and rise even higher. I realized I would have to react, and react fast. I knew that I couldn't sit stagnant or I would soon drown in this fire pit. There came a point where the heat from the flames began to make my hands sweat. I could feel my grip begin to slip. At that exact moment, the cliff from which I hung began to tremble. I pulled myself up just enough to look over top of the cliff. When I peered over the ledge I saw a stampede of people sprinting toward me and the edge of the cliff. There had to be billions of people running in this direction.

"What were they running from?" my dad interrupted.

Honestly while I was on the cliff I wondered the same thing. Then off in the distance I noticed a humongous, ugly dragon chasing the people. Moments later, one by one, these people began running and leaping off of the cliff, plunging to their deaths. I watched many people fall into these flames. I saw their bodies become engulfed in the massive of flames below. This went on for what felt like hours. What really baffled me about this whole thing was that it looked as if the flames weren't killing these people. There had to be billions of people swimming in these flames and screaming at the tops of their lungs. I could hear them screaming, and as I watched some of them reached for me. This is when I became petrified. How could I even be put into this situation? Picture me hanging on for dear life from the cliff with my legs swinging. I couldn't make sense of this. I ran on this mountain every day and I'd never seen anything like this. I tried to hoist myself to the top of the mountain, but my arms were completely numb. I tried my very best to raise myself, but nothing worked. Then I heard loud flapping sounds and saw the sky darkening. I looked up and saw an enormous swarm of black crows. Inside each crow's mouth were scorpions. The crows began to drop the scorpions from their mouths into the fire pit. You could hear each scorpion screeching in pain like the tires of a driver who has decided to break entirely too late. The crows hovered over the pit gazing at the screaming people and screeching scorpions. Moments later I heard a very loud finger snap sound. After this finger snap every crow fell from the sky and landed in the fiery pit. Now I was absolutely petrified of falling. I kept trying to pull myself up, but each of my attempts failed and my arms were getting more and more tired. They were almost completely numb and with every second that passed, my hands became sweatier and slid a little more. Next there was a very strong thumping that caused the cliff to tremble. With each thump delivered a thunderous sound. My hands began to tremble and my left hand swung off of the cliff. I was left hanging by one hand. I looked down at the treacherous flames, the screaming people, and I tried desperately to grip my feet to the side of the cliff. But my attempts to dig my feet into the cliff didn't work. Every time I tried to kick my feet up, they would slip from their position, releasing a cloud of dirt. Every second that passed the thumping got louder and more powerful. I then looked up and saw that the dragon stood above me. Looking into my eyes with infrared laser beam like pupils, it began to snap at me. It then exhaled a disgusting murky smoke from its mouth. The soot from the smoke covered my face and burned my eyes. Tears streamed from my eyes from the excruciating sting of the smoke. Suddenly I then heard a loud voice say, "Open your eyes." I didn't like the idea of this. I was afraid to see what waited in front of me. Again I heard the voice. "Open your eyes. See what's in front of you. If you want to be saved from this dragon and those flames, open your eyes. Listen to Me, I am the only way out of this."

So I obeyed the voice, opened my eyes and the dragon was still there snapping at me. But something felt different. I wasn't afraid of the dragon anymore. The voice that instructed me to open my eyes had so much warmth and love. It filled me with all the confidence that I needed to no longer be afraid of the dragon. Then I saw a bright flash and looked up to see the dragon being lifted. It was being lifted by an extremely powerful figure. This powerful figure then launched the dragon into the flames. Then I saw a burnished bronzed-colored hand reach for me. I looked up into His face, but I couldn't really see it. There was a magnificently powerful glow that projected off of His face. He asked, "Would you like me to save you?"

"Yes, please, save me!" I cried.

He said, "Acknowledge me for who I am, which is your Lord and Savior. Next I want you to acknowledge that your daily habit of mountain running is wrong. I also want you to turn from this habit and never do it again."

This left me with a decision to make. I could follow these instructions or I could burn in these flames. The decision was obviously a no brainer. So I asked Him to save me. I acknowledged Him as Lord and Savior. Next I acknowledged my wrong doings. After this He told me to pull myself up and over the ledge of the cliff. I explained that I had tried for hours to do just that, but my arms and legs were too tired. I told Him that in my weariness I just couldn't do it. I didn't have any strength left. He looked at me and placed His hand on my forehead. His next response was, "I give you renewed strength when I am in your presence. Now lift yourself up."

So I did just that. All of a sudden I was able to grip the cliff, and the sweat from my hands was dry. I pulled myself up over the ledge and onto the mountain. I collapsed as soon as I was on solid ground. I laid there happy with an overwhelming feeling of joy. I went over to Him and hugged Him. "How can I ever repay you?" I asked.

He said, "It's impossible to repay me, but there is one thing that I want you to do. I want you to pick up that dead body that's lying over there and throw it into the fire pit."

I looked down at the body and gasped, completely stunned. The dead body lying there was identical to mine – same exact face, clothes, and body. I asked, "Why do I have to throw the body?"

He said, "Because the moment I saved you, he died. This guy cannot live, if you are with Me. So it's either you live with Me, and he remains dead…or he lives and you both get thrown into the fire pit. The two of you cannot coexist."

This made complete sense to me at that moment. So I picked up the body that was identical to myself and threw it off of the cliff. It soared into the air and nose-dived into the fiery pit.

"Wow, that's amazing," my dad said.

"Yeah, tell me about it. That dreamed seemed so real!" I said.

He asked, "Son, do you know why that dream seemed so real? It's because it *was* real, this wasn't a dream." In disbelief I asked him what he meant by that.

His response was, "You see, here's what happened. It all started when…

To be continued!!!

The Cliffhanger

<u>Cliffhanger Break Down</u>

Sometimes in life we are like the guy hanging off the cliff. Some of us have these habits that are hardly conducive to the Will of God. Of course there are the obvious bad habits like various addictions, violent behaviors, and so forth. What about the habits that may not be so obvious? Like in the Cliffhanger, this guy ran the mountain daily and never saw it as a serious problem. That is until he couldn't slow down when he reached the edge of the cliff. As humans we sometimes have habits that are not of God. The overall message of this chapter is meant to stress the truth that Jesus is going to return soon. None of us knows when this will happen. There are many things that we indulge in on a daily basis that we shouldn't. Honestly, some of us don't realize the damage we are doing through these actions. But ignorance will never be a valid excuse. For the people who knowingly do things that God disapproves of, what's their reasoning? As a sinner myself, there are definitely habits or actions that I may have knowingly taken part in that were not of God. My reasoning behind them was probably the same as many of you readers. In my mind, I used to think, *Well Jesus probably isn't coming back soon, I'll have time to repent....He won't return in my lifetime.* As my relationship with The Lord began to strengthen, I learned just how preposterous my calculations were. As sinners we might think, *Hey there's always tomorrow to repent.* What I learned was that we shouldn't have this mindset for two reasons.

The first reason is that we can't possibly know when Jesus will return. It could be today, tomorrow, next year, next century. We don't know. We should live life like today is the day of His return. Before you make certain actions or react in certain ways, ask yourself one thing: If Jesus were to return right now, would you like for Him to catch you acting in your current manner? If your answer is No, that means that you need to make some adjustments in your life.

> *But of that day and hour no one knows, not even the angels of Heaven, but My Father only.* -Matthew 24:36

The second reason we should stop our negative actions is because of something called integrity. It's easy for us to act holy and righteous when we are at church. How about when no one is watching? Let's be mindful that God watches over us at all times and can read our hearts. Have integrity for who we are and what we represent at all times. Let's be prepared for the return of Jesus Christ before it even occurs. Let's always be ready, so we ever have to get ready. In Ephesians, it states that as a soldier in God's army this preparedness is actually a part of our uniform (Ephesians 6:15), and we should be prepared at all times; we never know when God's going to call on us

> *He who walks with integrity walks securely, But he who perverts his ways will become known.* -Proverbs 10:9

> *The integrity of the upright will guide them, But the perversity of the unfaithful will destroy them.* -Proverbs 11:3

Better is the poor who walks in his integrity
Than one perverse in his ways, though he be
rich. -Proverbs 28:6

And having shod your feet with the prepara-
tion of the gospel of peace. -Ephesians 6:15

If the world ended today, and it were time to head for the gates, what would your experience be? What would you like God to say? When our time comes, we should want God to welcome us into Heaven, unhesitatingly. Imagine how great it would feel for you to go to the gates and see God waiting for you with open arms, saying, "Welcome Home." We should all strive for this introduction. Let's work hard to live right by God. We don't want there to be any doubt upon our entry.

The Stampedes

As in the chapter, there will be billions of people chased into Hell by the devil. They will be joined by the devil's followers and worshippers who were symbolized by the scorpions, and they will be joined by the demonic spirits that were represented by the crows in the chapter. In the chapter, the scorpions were hovering over the fire pit from the mouths of the crows. Metaphorically this is illustrated in real life as well. The people who choose to support evil things (scorpions) are truly being led by demonic spirits. In this situation, these individuals are possessed and leave the control of their destiny in the hands of the demonic spirits (crows). Just like the crows in the dream, these demonic spirits know that their future will be spent in the pits of Hell for eternity. Their goal is to bring evil supporters (scorpions) with them.

The moment when God decides to send them and the devil to Hell, that's exactly where they will go. They will not be able to stop it. There was a part in the dream when the stampede started and the narrator was unsure about what caused it. This symbolized how in life there are some social norms that everyone appears to follow. Since these things are social norms, many people ignorantly believe that there is no problem with them. They then begin to follow the example of the people who are marching in front of them. Since the crowd is moving in a certain direction, many people feel they should too. This is because they don't want to be outcasts. They don't want to be different and run in the opposite direction. At what point do these people question, "What are we running towards?" Sadly enough, like the stampede of people in the dream, many people wait until it's too late to question where they're headed. They are ignorantly following the people in front of them who are running to the fiery pits. Some people don't understand what caused them to do certain actions until they see the big dragon running behind the crowd. Some people truly don't understand that they are supporting the acts of the devil. They just know that they're following what everyone else is doing.

Some of us are given an opportunity to change our lives instead of jumping into the fiery pits. God may show us mercy and give an opportunity to be saved while we're hanging at the edge of our spiritual cliffs. From that understand nothing "just happens." There's a reason you were able to grab the edge of the cliff – especially when billions of others weren't as fortunate and fell into the pit. God is giving you a second chance to change your ways. There is reason you survived your life-threatening disease. There is a reason you overcame your addiction. There is a reason you are standing after years of abuse. There is a reason you have been given a second chance to restore your damaged relationships. God has decided to save you for a reason. God has made you tough enough to overcome your circumstances. This journey will be anything but easy; you are going to struggle to get back on top of the mountain. However, with God you will reach the mountain top. Even though your arms are numb and weakened. You are still hanging on for a reason. As long as you're breathing, make the most out of your life. Try to get back to where God wants you to be.

The Last Body

In this chapter there's a part where the narrator is instructed to throw a body into the pit. This body is him. Well at least what used to be him. Bishop TD Jakes said it best, "You can't be who you used to be and who you're going to be at the same time." When we surrender our lives to Jesus Christ we are officially born again into a new spiritual body. A week before I actually wrote this chapter, I was presented with a test. Long story short, someone broke into my car while I was in a café meeting with a friend discussing this exact book. When I returned to my car I saw that my entire front seat had been trashed. I was instantly furious. I started up my car and drove around looking for this person. I admit that this wasn't the best idea. I wasn't as grounded in my faith as I should have been. So I drove up the street and I saw a car alarm going off. This let me know that the guy was still on the loose. I turned down a side street where there were a lot of cars parked. There were also quite a few people walking up and down the sidewalks. To my surprise I noticed a homeless man looking in many car windows and checking to see if their doors were unlocked. I watched this guy go to at least seven cars. When he got to the final car, I knew this was the guy. I pulled up to him and proceeded to confront him. I will be honest, I definitely handled this the wrong way – a way that God disapproved of. I shouted at the man using obscenities and threatened to violently harm him. As the entire street looked on, I yelled at the man, "*You're lucky that I gave my life to The Lord. A few years ago I would have done this...and would have done that...blah blah blah.*" On the car ride home I spoke to God and asked Him to forgive me for my actions. During this conversation, God told me that I definitely handled the situation wrong. Confronting the man wasn't the bad part, it was the way I confronted him that was wrong. Then God told me something that I will always remember. He asked me, "*Why did you say, 'Had this been a few years ago...I would have done this or that'...? This isn't a few years ago; stop mentioning who you used to be and how you would have responded. That person is dead and gone.*" That statement from God motivated me to focus on fixing my flaws. It motivated me to keep going in the direction that God wanted me to go. So that whole experience motivated me to write this part of the chapter with the dead body. I realized that I had to pick up the old me and throw him into the pit. Jesus died so that I could have life. So it was time that I lived for Him. In life we cannot live in the Kingdom of God and live by the ways of the world. We must make a decision.

> *Knowing this, that our man was crucified with Him, that the body of sin might be done away with, that we should no longer be slaves of sin. -Romans 6:6*

> *No one can serve two masters; for either he will hate the one and love the other, or else he will be loyal to the one and despise the other. You cannot serve God and mammon. -Matthew 6:24*

Reach for the hand

In life there are some of us who are hanging on the edge of that cliff. I am here to tell you that there is still time to grab ahold of that hand. The beautiful bronzed hand belongs to the one and only Jesus Christ. He wants you to reach out for Him and allow Him to save you from the fiery pits of Hell below. I want to encourage you to allow Him to enter your life. He is the only way. He is the only one who can save you from what you are going through. He is also the only one who can save you from the fiery pits of Hell. At this point in the book I am going to invite you to reach for the hand of Jesus. By doing this, you will be accepted into the Kingdom of God and will be saved from the pits of Hell. If you are interested in being saved, I would like you to recite the prayer below. Please recite the prayer out loud and this will classify you as being saved.

"Almighty God, I acknowledge the fact that I am a sinner and that my sins have distanced me from you. Lord, I am truly sorry for my sins and deserve to be punished. Today I accept Jesus Christ as my Lord and Savior. I believe that He died on the cross for my sins and then rose again. Please forgive me for my sins and help me turn away from my previous ways of living. I invite you, Lord into my heart. At this very

moment I vow to serve you to the best of my ability. Please save me. In Jesus Christ's name I pray, Amen."

If you sincerely said that prayer out loud, I would like to now officially welcome you to the Kingdom of God. May the grace of our Lord Jesus Christ be with you all. Amen.

Made in the USA
Lexington, KY
25 August 2017